The Local Economy Revolution
Has Arrived!

What's Changed

and

How You Can Help

Expanded & Updated

Della G. Rucker

A publication of Wise Fool Press

Published by Wise Fool Press, an imprint of the Wise Economy Workshop, LLC

3570 Sherbrooke Dr.
Cincinnati, Ohio. 45241 USA
www.wiseeconomy.com

Produced and printed in the United States of America.

ISBN Print Version: 978-0-9900044-9-3

ISBN EPUB Version: 978-1-7367072-0-3

Library of Congress Control Number: 2013951056

9 780990 004493

Dedication

It wasn't until I put this first version of this book together that I realized how much George Gott influenced my thinking, my work, actually pretty much everything. He would have never expected that. I assume that, somewhere in the universe, he knows that now.

Thanks, Dad.

Acknowledgements

One of the joys of my professional and personal life is that I have been able to share both with an incredible array of wise, fascinating and incredibly insightful people. This list is going to be incomplete, but I'll try.

Thanks to Bill Lutz and Peter Mallow, who were authors of the original content that make up parts of four of the chapters of this book. I twiddled their wording, and I cleaned up their grammar. But it was their content to begin with. I cannot thank those two smart guys enough.

Thanks to all of the community professionals, dedicated officials and awe-inspiring volunteers whom I have had the privilege of working with over close to 30 years. You show what it means to care about and fight for your place.

Thanks to the colleagues who have encouraged me, challenged me, and led me to believe that I might not be nuts. To Paul, Anatalio, Tammy, Martin, Jon, Kate, Jennifer, Jason and hundreds of others: my very deep gratitude.

Deep thanks to Deb Zwez, Rebecca Maclean, Kjirsten Frank Hoppe, Michael Hammes and all who reviewed draft copies of this first edition of this book or engaged in conversations about the essays that some of this book derives from on my blog and on LinkedIn. I'm grateful that so many have decided to care about what I said enough to help make it better.

Huge thanks to my kids, James and Jon, who have put up with my distractions and the times that I told them that they had to get their own butts to the rec center because it would be a waste of my time to drive them. And who also provided a surprising amount of the raw material in here. And also transformed my life by making me a mother. But they don't know much about that part yet.

And the deepest thanks to David, my husband of more than half my life, who enlightens me, expands my horizons, and inexplicably continues to put up with me. I've called him my secret weapon, and that he is. Love you, babe.

Table of Contents

Foreword

Change sucks.

None of us want to live in a world where the basic assumptions that we framed our lives and work and communities around have changed. Approaches that used to do what we wanted stop working, assumptions we used to rely on don't apply any more. Our carefully-guarded proverbial apple carts end up dumped all over the ground.

No wonder we often just want to stick our fingers in our ears and insist that everything's fine, we just need to wait 'til the good old days come back.

But in our guts, we all know: our communities are different now, very different. When whatever good times come back, if they come back, they're not going to look like what we had yesterday.

And frankly, that feels awful. And it especially feels awful if you take some responsibility for your community's economic health -- whether you're a professional economic developer or a public administrator, an elected official, a board member or simply one of those people who give a damn about the future of the place where you live.

It would be nice if the programs and incentives and tools and assumptions about people we've been using since the 2000s, or the 1990s, or the 1980s or earlier, still worked. After all, we know what they are, we know what they do. We like being able to point at simple success stories, cut ribbons, crow over the new factory. And that stuff makes our local economy better, right? Isn't that what we need?

But what about when they don't?

What about when it's not?

This book is here to help all of us who care about our local communities recognize what's changed, and to help us change how we respond to those changes. That's scary, and yes, sometimes it sucks. We'll try to deal with that.

At the end of the day, though, we don't have a choice. As I'll tell you in the next section, I've spent almost all of my life in the opening rounds of this sea change, the transition to the Fusion Economy or the Network Economy. It's affected pretty much everything I've encountered, both personally and professionally. It's past time to take the scales off of our eyes, own up to the way the world has changed and is changing, and get on with the job of the Local Economy Revolution.

The good thing is that people are doing that — people all over the country and all over the world. You'll meet some of them here. But we need more, a lot more.

So I hope you'll join us and grab that change by the horns. Perhaps more importantly, I hope that by the time you finish reading this thing, you'll know that this deep change is possible. And that you can help.

Vive la revolution. Let's go make it happen.

—

This book isn't a how-to manual. It's a collection of essays that come at the core issues from multiple angles.

That's because the world is still writing the

how-to-manual. We're still figuring it out.

But in order to figure it out, we need to understand what we are facing, what has changed and how we need to shift our base assumptions so that we can each contribute a couple of paragraphs to the new economy's how-to manual.

That said, this isn't a book for everyone. But it is a book for a lot of different ones.

If you work for a local or regional government or you have responsibility for a community-based nonprofit like an Independent Business Alliance or Main Street or a community development corporation, this book should give you some thinking tools. I hope it will allow you to look up from the fires you have to put out every day and the messes that seem to pile up on every side. I hope it will give you some tools to help you more productively reframe the big issues that are impacting your work and giving you those ulcers, and I hope it will give you some encouragement to make your difference in the face of the tough decisions and the seemingly no-win choices you increasingly face.

If you're an elected official or serving on a commission or board, I hope this will give you some new answers to some of your hardest questions - like, "Why isn't our economy getting better?" You'll discover that the answers have more moving parts, than you might have expected. And you'll also discover that you have a powerful role to play, although not the one you might have expected. And a wicked, but worthwhile, challenge ahead.

If you're a volunteer, an advocate, one of your community's People Who Give A Damn: you will probably discover that you have the most important role of all.

This book is asking your community to throw out many of the assumptions and methods they've been defaulting to for 30 years or more. People may know in their guts that this isn't working, but if they're in any kind of leadership position, that's a frightening situation.

If the folks you elected and the organizations you support advocate for deep change, and you're not clearly in their corner, I promise you that those who are benefitting from the current system, those who don't see the need for change...

Will make their lives very unpleasant.

They need you to advocate, to agitate, to raise pressure for a new way of making our communities better. So stand with them. Speak in support of them. Please.

Systemic change has never come from policies and legal opinions. It doesn't come from government staff or elected officials. It comes from us. If you want your community to thrive, it has to start with you. Now more than ever.

I hope this book will give you a framework for rethinking what your community's future should look and feel like, and some examples to indicate that this kind of deep change is possible. And maybe it will give you something that you can share with your electeds and appointeds and executive directors and the like, to help you say what you want to say.

But this book alone won't make that happen. If you don't advocate for this change, my voice is a violin in the void. As I'll say later, a violin in a void can have some power. But we need a lot more of them to fill the gaping space in front of us.

Enjoy. Thanks.

How to use this book

They say that you should write the book you want to read. I think I got as close to that as I can.

What I don't want to read is another analysis or how-to manual. *We've got a lot of those.* Thousands of white papers and blog articles and bits and pieces of what we ultimately need to do. And frankly, while much of that work may give us sound, important ideas, Too often they don't move the larger needle the way their authors would have liked.

> Tools are well and good, but if we don't know why we are using them, then we can end up repeating old mistakes with a new set of widgets.

They don't do that because they're *intellectual exercises.* They're tools. Tools are well and good, but if we don't know why we are using them, if we don't examine our purpose and assumptions and get clear on what exactly we're trying to accomplish, then we can end up repeating old mistakes with a new set of widgets.

More importantly, a tool can't resonate with our hearts, with the reasons why we try to do the hard things that have to be done. With our Purpose.

What I wanted to read was something that set those tools and bits in a broader context. Something that created a more complete picture of the framework that underlies the experiments and pilots and the white papers.

Maybe more importantly, I wanted something that wasn't a strictly left-brain read. Not an instruction book. Not a have-to.

I wanted something that you would read because you wanted to.

Something that gave you something worthwhile to think about in the shower or while walking the dog. Something that sparked meaningful conversations with your colleagues and friends.

Something that taps that place in your guts where the reason why you care, in the face of all those challenges, still lives.

Something you can read because it helps you do the work that Matters.

I also wanted something that required minimal commitment, since doing this work requires so much. My favorite authors have always been those who write anthologies -- collections of stories or essays. As a reader, you can finish a story or essay in one sitting, and you don't have to remember where you were in the story arc or who did what to whom last.

More importantly, I think an anthology approach is more relevant than ever. In this book, we are talking about multi-dimensional topics -- ecosystems, rather than machines, as I will say later. And writing or reading is an inherently linear task -- you start at the beginning and move through a logical procession to the end.

So instead of distorting the whole of these ecosystems by squashing them into one forced story arc, you might think of the parts in this book as collections of smaller stories that begin from a shared issue. You can picture each of the sections as Sputnik-type shapes, with a center orb and a bunch of long spikes coming off of the orb in every direction. The orbs are the Undercurrents in Part 1, or the Implications in Part 2, or the Secret Weapons in Part 3. And the individual chapters are different perspectives or angles or ways of understanding that first core issue.

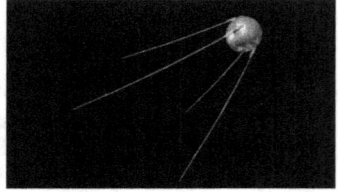
Sputnik. A ball with antenna.

By the time you finish this book, you're not going to know if Frodo went back to his village, or the Three Steps to Happiness and Weight Loss. But you will have a future-minded, nuanced, and multi-dimensional perspective.

And you will be as well equipped as anyone to help lead your Local Economy Revolution.

Who is this?

If I'm going to hit you with the challenges and opportunities facing our communities in this new era, maybe I'd better give you some idea where I'm coming from. As I'll say later on, making wise decisions depends on understanding the limits of the information you're working with. Might as well start by applying that to me.

I'm as much a product of the U.S. Rust Belt as anyone you'll meet. I grew up in a small town outside of Cleveland, Ohio, where my father and grandfather ran a small paint factory. The factory was a sort of jack-of-all-trades type establishment, making everything from primers to spray paints for wholesalers and retailers. In the pre-rusting Rust Belt, there was a lot of metal to protect, so the paint-making business kept about eight people, including my dad and grandfather, pretty busy.

Until about 1981. As a result of being where I was when I was, I had a front row seat for the first convulsions of the collapse of the traditional manufacturing economy. The collapse that's still playing out today.

By the time I was in middle school, several of the company's customers had gone out of business, and the market for a jack-of-all-trades paint manufacturer had collapsed. The company was sold for its assets (the only value left). My father was out of work for most of three years.

Thankfully, I had encouragement in high school, and I was able to go to a very good college. I ended up with an undergraduate degree from Northwestern University in Chicago and, about 10 years later, a Masters in Community Planning from the University of Cincinnati. So for the most part, I came out OK.

But I don't think my father ever got over those years. Unemployment isn't just a statistic in some government report — it's a life profoundly dislocated. You can't always control that, but do try not to forget that. OK? Thanks.

—

I have had four or five careers, depending on how you want to count. I sometimes joke that my career path looks like cooked spaghetti. I started out as a small town journalist, and then became an English teacher, which gave me a skill set for managing and guiding groups of people to find answers and meaning for themselves. It did not, however, give me much in the way of job prospects, since I came out of college in a place and time where there were five times more teachers than anyone needed.

As I tried to figure out my next act, I ended up with a consulting business that focused on historic preservation and downtown revitalization. Through a typically convoluted process, that work morphed into community planning, which morphed into economic development planning and swung back around to include community revitalization, public engagement and a little journalism. And then I started a couple more businesses and worked on higher education experiential learning and doing things that I had never heard of in Cleveland. Whoever said God has a sense of humor apparently had a hand in my resume.

And in the process I have had the great gift of working and caring and striving with many, many people who are not like me -- people whose cultural and racial and socio-economic and personal experiences taught me far more than I would have ever learned anywhere else. I

19

have had hundreds of teachers, and still do today. I will never be able to thank them enough for how they change and expand me.

At some point in the book, I will end up touching on all of those - and also on parenthood, a constant source of delight, frustration and total chaos. My personal narrative will also bounce geographically — Cleveland, yes, but also Cincinnati, where I live today, and Green Bay, Wisconsin, where I spent most of the 1990s. And assorted client locations, an occupational hazard when you've spent much of your adult life consulting with local governments.

Enough. Let's get on with it.

What's happened since 2013

I published the first version of this book in 2013, incorporating essays I had written as early as 2010. Not all that long ago, but...hey, it's been a long decade. And as I returned to the old version on occasion, I saw a lot of the content that still worked, but I felt like some important things were missing. That resulted in this update.

So, what's changed?

First, some of the simple things. Obviously, I'm older. My kids are older (both in college in 2021). Dave is older. And the people who wrote early versions of some of the chapters in this book have moved on to different careers. But that doesn't change the truth of what they wrote before.

The biggest changes are probably inside my head.

Like a lot of people, I find myself more cynical about the potential for national solutions to these challenges in a post - 2016 world. At the same time, I have a fragile, guarded optimism that important new solutions are developing that will lead us in a better direction.

A lot of what I hoped was around the corner in 2013 didn't happen as quickly as I thought it would. And the 2016- 2020 period made a lot of us realize that many of the core social elements that we had taken for granted, and that were necessary underpinnings for the progress this book is about, were a whole lot less certain than we thought. If I had been able to imagine the events of 2020 and early 2021, I don't know if I would have written this book back then.

I've learned that, on the individual level, the kind of change I've been talking about is even harder than I thought it would be. That's not just because of money or politics, but because of how our brains lock into our paradigms - our assumptions and expectations about How Things Work. Especially among those of us who have worked on a particular issue for a few years. As soon as you think you've got it figured out, *Surprise!* You've locked yourself into a box that makes it almost impossible to see what your assumptions about How Things Work are missing or got wrong.

I spent four years between 2013 and now working on a business where I had to throw out most of my previous assumptions about the *right* way to do something, anything, something as basic as talking to a client. That throwing out and rebuilding is one of the hardest things I've ever done. Worth it, but viciously hard in the process.

That experience gives me a bit more soberness about some of the hard things that this book may challenge you to do. And much more admiration for the people who take on those challenges.

What else? I've also written a few more books since then. *Crowdsourcing Wisdom* in 2015 was intended to give a how-to on doing the kind of hands-on, directly meaningful public involvement that I was advocating. It's used to teach classes for future planners in California. *Everyone Innovates Here* came out in 2018, and presents a new inclusion-powered model for designing innovation ecosystems -- a strategy that was heavily formed by my experience with Econogy in the late 2010s. And another book, tentatively titled *Public Engagement Done Right*, was written but withdrawn from the publisher when I realized that it would probably get lost in their system. So that will see the light at some point.

But I think this is the most important change since the first version of this book came out: In 2013, I understood that racism and inequity existed, but like a lot of us who have enjoyed privilege, I didn't really understand. I didn't recognize the structures underlying the damage that was being done to my Black friends. I didn't see the implicit biases, I didn't get how past barriers continue to live on and hamstring lives today.

I hope I've become a little more attuned, a little better ally, a little more understanding of the ways in which too many people have been left behind in a whole host of ways. And the more I learn, the more I understand how much I don't understand. I still screw up. A lot.

Perhaps more importantly, I've come to deeply appreciate how reaching out to include, to center, diverse perspectives give us our best opportunities for the kind of change we all need. It's still Important to do your homework and be brave, but more and more I find that crowdsourcing wisdom is our strongest secret weapon -- provided that we are crowdsourcing from as much of the full and rich and deep complexity of humanity as we can. And paying particular attention to the voices that have been left out before.

> I've come to deeply appreciate how reaching out to include, to center, diverse perspectives give us our best opportunities for the kind of change we all need.

Not to be nice, but because we need them. Really need them.

Not just because of morals or ethics or a sense of

Supposed To, but because those voices that have been left out have the best chance of helping all of us understand what the conventional leaders have missed by getting stuck in their own boxes.

Finally, my writing style has evolved a bit. When I wrote the content of the first version in the early 2010s, I was trying to re-discover my real voice after a couple of decades of churning out mind-numbing professional blah blah blah. In some cases, I think I trended a little too goofy, a little too harsh, a little too... something. Or maybe I've just mellowed. Who knows. So I reserve the right to put an extra polish on the occasional clunker.

Enough. As I said back then, Let's get on with it.

The Local Economy Revolution First Principles

In 2010, I left a Big Engineering Firm to start my own practice.

I was frustrated. I knew there were things that mattered a lot to me that staff in Big Engineering Firms don't get to do, and I'd reached a point where that conflict couldn't continue if I wanted my brain to stay in one piece.

By that point, I had worked with communities across the U.S. doing assorted kinds of planning for a lot of years. I'd stood in places that were thriving, and I'd walked with staff and residents through places that were collapsing. From what I saw and what I knew about economies, planning, organizations and psychology, I found myself advocating for a deep-seated reset to how we organize and carry out the work of managing our communities, convinced that the needs were bigger than a new social enterprise or a new grant program.

So I wrote a thing called the Wise Economy Manifesto, and in it I tried to encapsulate what I was thinking. And it seemed to make sense to people. But over the decade since I first did that, I've been working and learning in a lot of different spaces, and I realized that this statement needed to incorporate those lessons.

I've reframed it here as the First Principles of navigating this new and emerging era in ways that lead us to more future-ready cities.

How to use the Local Economy First Principles

A set of First Principles isn't a how-to guide. It's not a checklist, it's not a Do- These-Three- Things- To-Lose-Lots-of-Weight piece that promises a super easy way to do something super hard.

First Principles are a framing of the big issues, the priorities, the beliefs or ethics. Taken together, they are a foundation rock, something that you use to hold up and make stable the things you build upon it. Taken individually, statements of First Principles can seem self-evident, and occasionally pompous, because the point of a statement of First Principles is to lay out that framing in absolute and unambiguous terms.

That doesn't mean you should memorize it, catechism-style. That would be weird.

But as you evaluate your ideas for your community (or the ideas or programs that get presented to you as Of Course This Is What We Should Do), you can refer back to this section as a reminder of what you are really seeking -- and a tool for evaluating whether what you're planning to do is really in alignment with where your community needs to go.

The Driving Force

- **Welcome to the Fusion Economy. Time to put the Industrial Era behind us.** This is the uber-issue, the thing that makes every other item here not just a nice-to-have, but crucial, imperative. We're getting left behind by ourselves. The transition we're currently making isn't between an Internet 2.0 and Internet 3.0 economy, or between an Information Economy and something else. It's much more profound and pervasive than that.

We're still too much stuck in the Industrial Era, especially in how we structure organizations, government, public programs and businesses, and especially in terms of how we manage people in any of those settings. But emerging technologies and societal expectations and new ways of working are pulling us, sometimes dragging us, into a new place, which I've taken to calling the Fusion Economy.

Many of our most violent struggles come from the deep mis-matches between the basic operating paradigms underlying those two economies. A lot of what we did before didn't really work very well, or didn't work well for everyone. But because we were thinking in Industrial Era logic, we too often didn't notice. Now they work worse than ever. And we don't have that excuse anymore.

Rethinking Our Purpose

- **It's not about buildings or spaces or even, really, economics. It's about people.** We know that, we know, but... we don't. We say we're building a street or a program or a product for people, but too often our plans don't do what they were intended to do, or fix what they were intended to fix. But we pretend we don't see that, and we move on to the next one.

Part of the problem is that we hold regular people at arm's length from the process when they could potentially make it much more effective. But more importantly -- and more problematically -- we love the thing more than the people.

We say that we are designing and building our thing for people, but we get wrapped up in, obsess over, fall in love with the thing we've built, with its supposed beauty, simplicity, ideals, materials. We can easily do this with business ideas, and we definitely do this in architecture and urban design and historic preservation and public policy.

Why? For the same reason that we use babies and puppies to sell products. Because it's easier to love the simple, the unambiguous, the not-yet-compromised, than it is to love messy, complicated, not-always-predictable people. Or places made for and by people.

Or let those unwashed mess up our masterpiece.

But when we make it about something other than people, when we fall in love with the thing we made ostensibly to help them, we shouldn't be surprised when our creations make the lives of the people we thought we were helping worse, instead of better. Again, we've done that a lot during our Industrial Era upbringing. But we can't pretend anymore that we don't know any better.

- **Human communities are human ecosystems.** Everything we do, whether a business or a land use plan or a nonprofit program or an economic development incentive, isn't going to stay in the silo where we put it. We want to picture the world around us as working like machines, input -> predictable output, because that gives us some sense of optimism that we can predict what our work will cause. But that doesn't happen.

Instead, human communities are like forests and oceans and prairies. They are systems of interconnected systems (growth and decomposition, weather and weathering, hunter and prey), and what happens to one system impacts the others. And when we mess up one of them, it has an impact on everything else. That impact is often an unintended consequence of what we did. We know that. We have decades of science on this.

But because we don't do a good job of transferring those learnings to human ecosystems, we make new unintended consequences all the time. And we don't just *fail* to anticipate the unintended consequences of our work, we *purposely don't go looking* for them. We could see them if we looked for them, because we have lots and lots of examples to learn from. But we don't. By not critically examining how our systems impact each other, we permit wide and deep, and often unintended, repercussions -- repercussions on real people. Who, again, are supposed to be the ones we're doing this for.

- **We need to cultivate our native economic species.** The thing that grows naturally where you are can, with a little help and protection, provide more long-term benefit (and fewer of those unintended repercussions), than the exotics that we try to transplant at great cost. In this era, the

29

chase after the flashy, the big, the long shot, is too costly and too risky to deserve the lion's share of our attention.

This means that we have to focus on our assets instead of just our deficits. We're used to seeing signs of deficits -- vacant buildings, left-out people, failed businesses, organizations that struggle to pay their staff. We interpret those as meaning that something is broken, something requires an influx of money, experts, programs, to fill that deficit. And often, something new and more is definitely needed.

But what if at least part of the solution comes from the very things we assumed were deficits? What if we really dug into and valued and built upon the left-out people, and the unique things they are able to do? What if we used those vacant buildings to enable new ways of working and creating that build upon the intrinsic value of those assets, not just what we think they should be?

What could we create, uniquely, right here, with this and these, that hasn't been created yet?

After all, that which makes you unique makes you valuable. There is little value in being a commodity, but much opportunity in a well-defined niche.

- **White (elite) saviors fail most of the time.** I use that phrase mostly for the historic reference. You can replace "White" with "Elite," because non-white elites often fall into the same trap.

The White Savior trap is believing that because We

have more education, experience, money, connections, whatever, that We need to give or teach or instill or demonstrate something to Them - the people who don't have it. We may be well intended, but this assumption is one of the core causes of the failures we have seen in attempts to improve standards of living, economic involvement, etc. all over the world.

The truth is that We don't really have anything that special. At least not special enough to go all Lone Ranger and think we can shove ourselves into a different human ecosystem and not create at least as many new problems as we bring benefits. They, it turns out, often know how to work in their local environment, whether a savannah village or a car-dominated suburb, in ways that outsiders don't know.

Or won't try to hear or learn about, which is another problem that We often bring into the situation when We believe we have all the correct answers. Just because I have a big cape and an exotic accent doesn't mean that I understand your community. If I am not working in partnership with you, co-creating with you, you should kick me out.

- **Inclusion is not just a moral good, but a vast untapped resource.** We treat Talent (the kind that economic developers chase after) as though it were a rare metal. More and more businesses and communities are pursuing a pool of people that isn't growing that much, and a lot of them are competing at a big disadvantage to the few communities where those supposed Talent unicorns seem to want to go.

Talent is not a unicorn. It lives among us right now. Often it's not developed well enough for us to see it. Or it's in the wrong place, or has a color or a shape that we don't recognize. It may be rough around the edges, it may talk funny, it may be unsure what it can do or whether it can do it because it's been told so many bad things about itself.

But that kind of Talent may also be able to see opportunities that the pampered unicorns missed. And they're less likely to leave when the enticements run out. And they're more likely to fight through the tough times, because they have deep roots in the place and more than just economic motivations for making it work.

We have to have much better development of our overlooked Talent, especially the Talent from communities that don't have the same background and experience as the current tech world leaders. Then we will be able to truly create new and transformative stuff.

Rethinking the work of creating resilient communities

- **Change requires more than a lever. It requires a system.** Impact, even on something relatively simple like getting healthy food to a neighborhood, requires system thinking, not just doing stuff.

Too often, well-intentioned people think that if we just do this One Thing (build a grocery store, recruit a Big Business, revitalize the riverfront, build an Innovation Hub, whatever they think that means), then Magic Will Happen.

But we have a lot of people doing those One Things in more or less isolation, and that has given us a disjointed landscape where a huge amount of energy is being expended for often unimpressive results.

Most of the time, the One Things don't live up to their billing because we *assumed* that X would cause Y, without carefully defining and working on the intervening steps necessary to convert a new resource to desired outcome. Instead of making the assumption that X will cause Y, we need to walk carefully through the steps that will be needed to get from X to Y. Preferably in full partnership with the people who are already living in the space between those letters. And preferably with a careful eye out for the potential unintended consequences that can develop from intervening in a human ecosystem.

- **Entrepreneurial Mindset is the unmet need. For everyone.** When we ask people to self-manage multiple career changes, play an active role in improving their communities, do the hard work of continuous education, advocate for their children in school, we are basically asking them to live entrepreneurially. And what evidence there is indicates a multi-decade decline in entrepreneurial mindset in the United States. That's not surprising, given that the Industrial Era didn't want the millions of people who were working on their lines to upset their carefully-crafted systems. But the Fusion Era isn't accepting that.

In a situation where the old systems no longer work, to not be entrepreneurial is to be helpless - whether you are starting a business or not. You have to be able to see and capitalize on new opportunities. That goes for everyone, no matter your education level or profession or position or wealth. But most people have had few chances to experience,or exercise, an entrepreneurial mindset, because the Industrial Era didn't want it.

If our work is about people, and if we are so dependent on our Talent, then it falls out that an entrepreneurial mindset is arguably our biggest asset, our human ecosystem's new superpower. If we have lots of people who can think and act entrepreneurially, then we will have lots of good problem-solving and creation.

But to have that, we can't treat entrepreneurialism as this special playground for the wealthy or highly educated. Entrepreneurial work is everyone's work, if for no other reason than because non-entrepreneurialness is a recipe for deterioration. And that means that our budgets, our programs, our systems have to increase entrepreneurialism, especially for those who have been cut out of the game in the past.

- **Crowdsourced wisdom is the best way to find a real solution.** Perhaps the biggest learning of the Industrial-Fusion economy issue is this:

- The old ideas aren't working well and are mostly getting clunkier,

- We need all the bright ideas that we can get.

Guess what? Our communities are full of those bright idea sources. They know things, important things that we don't. We need them.

But impactful creativity requires some constraints. Just like water needs to be guided into a channel before it can drive a turbine, we have to create environments where that insight and creativity and entrepreneurial mindset can make a productive impact.

Short version: An open mic in the middle of the room, or a Facebook page, or a customer service bot, ain't gonna cut it.

- **Most important issues exist on a continuum, not a binary choice.** We drop easily, far too easily, into Us vs. Them. Into Right and Left. Socialist and Reactionary. But let's be practical: in a human ecosystem, where the best solutions might fall completely outside of our own limited experience, approaching issues this way is like trying to build a house with no more tools than a hammer and a screwdriver. It's tying a hand behind our back and then wondering why we can't unravel a giant snarled knot.

Regardless of your belief system, a two-sided point of view is probably hiding more from you than it's showing. And we can't afford that loss of information anymore.

- **Beware the magic pill.** We all want easy answers; we all want there to be a simple solution.

  There isn't one.

  We have to get used to that, and commit ourselves to incremental, complex, messy change.

- **We who intend to help our communities thrive better be ready to be brave.** We have to reconnect to the reasons why we got into this, before the rules and bureaucracy and politics took over our field of view. Whether we want to or not, we are going to be on the front line of the fight for new solutions, and we are going to be useless if we are just punching the clock or wandering from election to election, or cool idea to new cool idea.

  We have to critically re-assess our professions and organizations and roles, and find the fortitude to break through the walls that are keeping our communities from being successful. We cannot be foolhardy, and we must admit that we don't have all the answers. But we have to be brave enough to help lead the expedition.

Part 1: Welcome to the Sea Change

What's changed?

What hasn't? Duh.

That things have changed is not breaking news to you. And we sense, although we don't always acknowledge, that the changes run much deeper than we might initially see.

But what are those changes? And what are those changes'going to mean for how we live and work in the communities we care about?

Our national media and conversations usually focus on Macroeconomics - monetary policy, stock market indices, international trade, national debt and stimulus powers, etc. And we certainly know that those issues aren't abstract, that they have real, albeit sometimes indirect, impacts on what we can or cannot do at the local level. Pre-2016, I had the mistaken impression that a lot of privileged people did, that the national scene could sort of take care of itself. We got that one wrong.

But in this book, I'm not so interested in whether one financial index is rising or falling, or what the bond yield looks like. Those issues have definite impacts, but they can also fool us. It can be easy for us to turn them into red herrings, siphoning away the energy that we need to invest in solving local-scale problems.

Because the real question isn't whether stuff will happen. Stuff will certainly happen. The question is, how do we set our communities up to thrive in a world of Macro Uncertainty. Macro Uncertainty has defined the last 30+ years and will be one of the defining factors of the Fusion Age.

What I am most interested in are the overlooked impacts that are playing out in communities in the U.S. and across the world. Impacts that are part of the fundamental reshaping of how our economies and communities work. Impacts that no one, no government, no organization, fully controls. Impacts that will fundamentally shape our communities' futures, regardless of whether the value of the dollar or the stock market rises or falls.

And since my objective here is to write something that you can use as a thinking tool, I'm going to pull down my focus to three core issues - let's call them **Undercurrents**:

- The fact that a community's economic success, today and into the future, depends on a lot of factors that were never "economic development" before. And that those factors are all tangled up with each other. I talk about this in the section called **"Economic Ecosystems."**

- The fact that we have a long, unaddressed history of creating unintended consequences - often very nasty ones - as a result of overly simplistic and know-it-all approaches to community economic challenges. I talk about this in the section called **"Unintended Consequences."**

- The fact that Talent is our new economy's raw material, and the kind of Talent we need in this emerging Fusion Economy increasingly does not look, act, respond or participate the way many of us think it should. I talk about this in the section called **"Talent: Not what we**

thought it was. Much more"

I told a story before about my family's small paint factory in the 1970s and 1980s Rust Belt, and that wasn't just an exercise in pulling off old scabs for amusement.

The lesson of the 1980s in Cleveland and many other places was that sea changes will impact us, and like the sea those changes are huge, complex and beyond our direct control. There wasn't one thing that put my family's factory, or a thousand others, out of business. There wasn't one thing that kept my father, or thousands of others, out of work for years and economically damaged for a lifetime.

That happened because of a combination of factors, ranging from short-sighted management decisions to new technologies in several industries. Welcome to chaos theory at work.

> What matters to me, and what I hope matters to you, is how we can most effectively equip the communities we care about for the unpredictable future coming down the road.

Changes in the larger world of global trade, generational preferences, technology and all that interrelated welter are happening and will continue to happen, and I think it's a fool's game to try to make big predictions about how those will play out over coming years and decades. As I said previously, one of the hallmarks of the Fusion Economy is turning out to be High Uncertainty. When you think you've got it figured out, chances are you got it at least part wrong.

What matters to me, and what I hope matters to you, is how we can most effectively equip the communities we care about for the unpredictable future coming down the road.

———

That sea change concept that I threw out in the title of this chapter probably needs some unpacking, especially if you're like I was until I married a guy who lives to sail. Because it's a central metaphor for what we're trying to do.

When you are captain of a sailboat -- whether it's the Sunfish that my kids learned to sail on, or an America's Cup catamaran -- what you can do and where you can go is constrained by the wind and the water. And the first lesson of sailing is:

If the wind is coming straight from the direction you want to go, you can't go directly there.

A sailboat always has to move at an angle to the direction of the wind. If you point the bow of the boat into the wind, you stop moving. So if the place you want to get to is in the same direction that the wind is coming from, you cannot just go there. You have to "beat," which means to go back and forth at an angle to the wind, zigzag-style.

You might say "damn it, I am going to go straight *there!*" You can try as hard as you want, but it ain't gonna work. Your only choices are to beat upwind, or go somewhere else. And if the wind direction changes, as happens about every 30 seconds on the little lake where we often sail, you have no choice but to change either your tactics or your plans about as often.

So there's wind. Water changes, too. If you're on the southeast shore of Lake Michigan, and a storm is coming from the northwest out of Canada, the wind will pile up the waves across the whole lake. By the time it gets to your harbor where you're trying to get your little piece of flotsam in the water, those waves look like mountains. You can have a lovely sunny day with a perfect wind, but those waves mean you're stuck... unless you change to a bigger boat, or change your destination.

Not so many people learn how to sail anymore. If we did, maybe we would learn to rely less on command and control approaches to our communities, and pay more attention to how we can shift to work with the sea changes in the world around us.

The rest of this section will outline some of those sea changes. After that, we'll look at some basic principles for how we might better navigate these waters.

Undercurrent 1:

Economic Ecosystems

Economic Ecosystems

If we're going to dive in, you might as well start at the deep end of the pool.

Let's think for a few minutes about the underlying bases of our assumptions about how our local economies and communities work. Because if we're going to enable the changes we need, we're going to have to rebuild from the foundations. We need to fundamentally change how we think about communities, businesses, organizations and governments.

We need to recognize that economic vitality depends on the health of a community, and that a community is not a set of separate, unrelated systems – a business district, a school system, a park system, a street system -- but an *ecosystem*. How our businesses do, what happens to our downtowns, what our parks look like, where we spend our money, how we talk about our communities... all that stuff doesn't just affect that one thing. It affects everything and everyone, especially the people whose participation we need the most.

We're starting to talk about the importance of "quality of life" as not just a planning function, but as a lynchpin of economic growth. But the lip service we've been giving to that topic doesn't go nearly far enough. We haven't fully internalized or changed our practices to address that interdependence, one of the most critical ramifications of

We create tons of unneeded pain and squandered opportunity for our communities simply by not thinking beyond our own pet interests or our own department walls.

"quality of life:"

We create tons of unneeded pain and squandered opportunity for our communities simply by not thinking beyond our own pet interests or our own department walls. This lack of interdependence acceptance is, at its core, one of the fundamental issues that stymies efforts to grow resilient communities today.

———

Economic development isn't *really* about just increasing the number of businesses or the number of jobs. We all know that.

The reason why communities do economic development, why they invest time and resources in it, is to make sure that the local economy has what it needs and is doing what it is necessary to support the health of the overall system. The purpose of economic development, at its core, is to help the community become stronger by making sure that the economic part of the ecosystem is fulfilling its role adequately.

Here's the hard truth, though: it's a hell of a lot easier to define our community's economic development work, and to trumpet our achievements, if we cast that work in terms of "winning new businesses" instead of "facilitating the health of the local economy."

It's a lot easier to count new jobs, or new employers, or hits on the web site, or hands shaken at the International Shopping Centers Conference, than it is to evaluate whether we are actually creating a healthier local economy. That is, unless we have a clear plan and are measuring the right kinds of improvements.

We *can* certainly do a clear plan and accurate measurements—there are a lot of resources out there that can help us do that.

The big barrier isn't technique. The big barrier is that meaningful action and evaluation to determine if you're actually improving the local economy takes more honest thought and stronger leadership than just chasing anything that moves and claiming every minimum wage job as a "victory."

> **Food for thought:**
>
> Who does your group or program *never* work with?
>
> What might these walls between you and they be hiding from you?

Because it's hard and takes leadership, we too often count the web site hits and handshakes, we shoot what flies and claim what falls, and assume (or take on faith) that our achievements are somehow supporting the community's ecosystem. But we never ask how, or check whether that's really happening. And then we wonder why it seems like the big picture never gets better.

We are all starting to figure out that "quality of life" has something important to do with the ability to grow a local economy. But until our understanding of the interdependence of the economy on the rest of the community ecosystem takes root, it's going to be far too easy to default to old measures — measures that often hide whether our efforts are helping the larger community or hurting it.

I pick on economic development a lot — and one of the goals of this book is to change how we see economic development work, whether we're professionals in that field or not. But the truth is that there is more than enough blame to spread around.

When urban planners assume that a bike lane system will have a "catalytic" effect on the local economy, or when elected officials through all their hope and weight behind a sports stadium, or even sometimes when residents fight a proposal because it will change a place's "character"...

It's the same error at work: we are not fully thinking about the entire ecosystem.

> It's easier to say "My stuff is important, yours isn't" than to try to look rationally at the whole range of issues and understand how My Stuff fits into the whole system.

People who do not have good economic prospects or are insecure about their jobs may use the bike lanes out of necessity, but may not shop in the stores by the bike lane like we anticipated especially if rents go up. People displaced by the stadium may not have another safe place to go, and oversized tax incentives may mean that there is less general fund monies available to increase the amount of safe affordable housing. And changing the "character" of a place might actually improve it, especially if it allows a more vibrant mix of people to use it. But that might not be the "character" that the earlier residents want.

We oversimplify the ecosystem, we stay in our silos and stick to our simple solutions, because it's intellectually easier. It's easier to say "My stuff is important, yours isn't" than to try to look rationally at the whole range of issues and understand how My Stuff fits into the whole system.

If we pretend that we don't have to worry about those

overlapping or contradictory impacts, if we pretend that our communities are nice simple frontier towns with lots of empty land to absorb those impacts and a small group of people to accommodate, then perhaps we can continue to pretend it's all simple. After all, if we screw it up too badly, we can move out into the scrub another five miles and start over. All we need are new subdivisions, right?

We made exactly that assumption in the second half of the 20th century. And it basically worked, until we ran out of empty land, or until those people that we were trying to accommodate become more numerous and more complicated.

That's where we are today.

If we are honest about the complexities of our communities, then we have to be honest about the fact that there are few, if any, simple solutions. Economic development issues don't just impact businesses, and when we don't see these related impacts, we will certainly feel their effects. If we want to facilitate the health of the ecosystem, we have to work on a wide range of elements in concert.

Ideally, this is what planning of any stripe should do, whether economic development strategic plans or community comprehensive plans or any other variant on the theme. It's part of why it becomes increasingly important to plan for multiple possible futures – with this many moving parts, a certain level of uncertainty is inescapable. But too often we only plan for My Stuff, not for the role our bailiwick plays in the larger system.

———

We are increasingly learning that natural ecosystems,

well, they're pretty cool. All those interconnections and interdependencies between the plants, the bugs, the animals and all give a strong ecosystem the same traits that we desire in our communities: long-term growth, healthy organisms, the ability to bounce back from disasters. Visit the site of a forest fire that happened three years ago, and you'll see what I mean.

And the biologists and botanists and other –ologists tell us that ecosystems that lose key members, like an animal that is part of the food chain, are bound for trouble or collapse. Even if that animal isn't featured on World Wildlife Federation bumper stickers.

> We need to think of our communities as economics-driven ecosystems, systems where the silo walls have broken down and where the leaves of one aspect of the community shade the roots and feed the animals that make up the rest of the system

If we are serious about building communities that are robust, resilient, flexible and don't leave us up a creek in the future, we need to think of our communities as economics-driven ecosystems, systems where the silo walls have broken down and where the leaves of one aspect of the community shade the roots and feed the animals that make up the rest of the system.

Resilience

Growing up in the Cleveland snow belt, plants weren't much on my radar... except for that first crocus of the year.

It came up at a time when spring was still imaginary and the black crust along the roadways made you think more of something dead than something coming back to life. Despite blizzards, despite ice, despite unending leaden grey skies, that impossible little patch of color came back year after year.

From wikimedia.org, subject to Creative Commons license.

There is something audacious, even ridiculous about a crocus. Tiny, flimsy little thing with its blossom too big for its stem, pushing in when larger and prettier plants won't grow, and taking on the same battle year after year.

Crocuses: nuts.

—

What do we want, truly want, for the communities that we care about? It's fair to say that we want them to be healthy – to thrive and succeed for the long term. No one goes into this work wanting to make short-term wins that will set the community up for disaster down the road. And even with our best efforts, we know that blizzards and long stretches of black snow will probably show up in the future.

What we really want, then, is to build *resiliency* – to equip our communities to bounce back from setbacks. We want them to overcome lost businesses and political fights and bad development decisions and continue to provide great places for people to live and work and all that other stuff we talk about.

But here's the kicker: resilient isn't flashy. Resilient usually isn't dinner-plate-sized blossoms, neon colors, explosive growth, front-page news.

> Resilience requires the right fit with the environment it's in, with all its limitations and dirty snow and lack of sunlight.

Community resilience requires careful attention to issues like business mix and diversity, places for many different kinds of people to live, plentiful options for getting around, systems for food and water and travel and people's livelihoods. Resilience requires strategies and systems that mitigate the risks, lowering the odds of a catastrophic blow.

—

About the time I became aware of the crocuses, the economy where I grew up was falling apart. We in the Rust Belt had learned to depend on a few industries, a few leaders, a few simple assumptions about the world, and we concluded that things would go on that way forever.

They didn't.

Cleveland today is a different place than it was in 1980 – better in some ways, more challenged in a lot of others, but on many measures, a place facing much harder times than it used to. If we'd had our eyes open, if we would have lessened our dependence on those few industries, leaders and assumptions, maybe things would have been different. Maybe, at least, we could have weathered the blizzard better.

Food for thought:

Is your favorite program or event helping make your community more *resilient*?

How?

Could you prove that?

A resilient community might not make a Million Places to See Before You Die list. It might not feature the showplace blossoms or the tallest stems, and it might look pathetic on your dining room table. But if what you really want is a place that lasts, a place that people will care about and care for through generations...if you want your community to be able to bloom again after the winter...perhaps we should take a closer look at that crocus.

Maybe it's on to something.

Paradigm Mismatch

As I've said before, anyone who was hanging out in the Rust Belt in the 1970s knows that the problems of decline and wage deterioration and disinvestment and economic inequity didn't drop out of the sky in 2008 or 2016.

So, so many of our community policies, our institutions and programs and organizations -- and perhaps more importantly, the assumptions that we built them on -- are simply mismatched to the needs of a new world and a new economy. Online yelling matches offered up as political debate? Tax systems based on a 19th century farming economy? Economic Development models of "winning" while our neighbors-- to whom we all know we are really joined at the hip -- suffer? Promised solutions that oversimplify the divergence and messiness of the humans that are supposed to live in these places?

> The most profound observations require someone or a group of someones to break through the unexamined assumptions that underpin the status quo.

You don't have to have an economics degree to see that in many cases, however you define it, something is not right.

Thomas Kuhn wrote years ago that the most critical scientific discoveries, the most profound observations, require someone or a group of someones to break through the unexamined assumptions that underpin the status quo. Because those assumptions are unexamined, we don't always see them. They are literally invisible in plain sight.

Those limitations stay in place until we figure out how to see them in a new way, or we encounter someone who is coming into the situation from somewhere else -- someone who can see where our barriers lie and doesn't believe in their legitimacy. Real breakthroughs often require entirely new thinking.

What does that have to do with you, your business, your local government, your job, your community?

Everything.

It means that each one of us who wants to make things better, who wants to build a better future, has to find ways to either bring out or be the conduit for that new thinking, for the way to find a new approach.

Yes, I know that you report to someone, have a budget, have responsibilities, don't want to rock the boat too badly. No one said you had to trade in your pants for camel's hair and eat locusts.

> **Food For Thought:**
>
> Look for the *walls* of your community's, your profession's, your organization's paradigm. What do you assume without question?
>
> Think about what you and your peers are assuming, and what the alternatives might look like.

Instead, may I give you a gentle encouragement to start looking for the walls of your community's, your profession's, your organization's paradigm. Think about what you and your peers are assuming, and what the alternatives might look like. Talk to people who have a different perspective -- who come from other communities, other types of organizations and jobs. They might not want to rock your boat either, but there's no harm in pushing on those walls a little... and see what you can learn.

We will talk more about how utterly important it is to co-create with people who are outside our own paradigm walls when we get to the third Undercurrent about Talent.

Gorilla Ecologies

Here's the question that extends from the paradigm shift we've been talking about:

What can we who work with cities and towns and neighborhoods do to build better, more resilient community ecologies?

One of the implications of that previous chapter is that we need to broaden the definition of the types of people we work with — and to do that, we often look for leaders.

Many of our communities depended on the support of a relatively small group of 800 Pound Gorillas who, whether elected or not, basically ran the town.

I probably don't have to tell you that those 800 pound gorillas are mostly extinct.

A lot of us know that we had predecessors who worked hand in glove with The Leaders Of The Community — we have black and white pictures in the hallway of our offices of serious-looking men in suits and horn rimmed glasses sitting around the boardroom table or cutting a ribbon somewhere.

And if we know our community's history, we might even know about the things that they did to make stuff happen — new highways, big developments, big factories. Big Stuff. Read a local history, and even if you manage to mentally strip out the common booster heroism in the stories, you'll see that in many communities, there was a small group of people who Got Stuff Done.

We got lazy in the 20th century in a lot of ways, but

one of them that we don't always talk about is that we got used to assuming that someone else would take care of us. That might have been the City Fathers, the Big Business that employed everyone (presumably for life), the Big Philanthropists who put their names on the library and the ball field. Many of our communities depended on the support of a relatively small group of 800 Pound Gorillas who, whether elected or not, basically ran the town.

I probably don't have to tell you that those 800 pound gorillas are mostly extinct.

I spent time recently working with a classic Rust Belt city, where we had a variant of a conversation that I have had more times than I can count:

In this community's history, the 800 Pound Gorillas consisted of the (mostly) men who owned the major factories. Need to raise money for a project? Need new people on City Council? Need to set priorities, kick someone into gear, make something happen? As long as you could get their attention (and you were willing to do it their way), it would happen. Stuff Got Done.

In this community, as in hundreds of others, the 800-pound gorillas are gone. Why doesn't matter - it's that combination of local and national and international forces at play. But it's water under the bridge now. Instead, this community has a large number of smaller players – 100-pound or 50-pound gorillas, if you will. Smaller businesses, smaller organizations, smaller pots of money. More leaders serving out of town corporations, with a stake in the place but not the deep roots that the old gorillas used to have. More people from different backgrounds, genders, races, interest groups. Fewer suits and horn rimmed glasses

It's not just that the obvious sources of money and leadership have dried up, which they have. One of the most powerful impacts of the sea change they have experienced is that it's nowhere near as simple to get the community's capacity in motion as it used to be. When we had that small, manageable group of gorillas to do our heavy lifting, we didn't have to think too hard about how to get them to work together. They just sort of did it, and we often didn't ask how.

> One of the most powerful impacts of the sea change they have experienced is that it's nowhere near as simple to get the community's capacity in motion as it used to be.

One of the key challenges that this community and others like this face is that we don't know how to harness the gorillas together. And this new group of gorillas doesn't automatically know how to do it themselves. So we underestimate the capacity we actually do have, we decry the loss of the Good Old Days, and we assume that we are stuck, that we can no longer make our communities better.

Like so many of these issues, we have to evolve beyond seat-of-the pants assumptions and the rules for playing together that we learned in elementary school. If we are going to help the communities we care about develop better economies, we are going to have to do so in a world where we can't be passive, where we cannot simply rely on someone with big muscles and deep pockets to do it for us. We have to actively engage the full range of smaller gorillas, help them learn to work together, and help them find ways to harness themselves together.

That's a different role for people who care about a community -- ringleader rather than supplicant -- but it's a role that we have to step into. Stepping into that role means that we have to:

- **Look for the overlooked or historically left-out gorillas.** As we learned in the Local Economy First Principles, diversity isn't just a moral issue, it's crucial to being able to identify and create legitimately new solutions. We get to new ideas most efficiently and effectively when we have people in the process who do not see the situation from the conventional perspective. And what we need most are variations from, or even total breaks from, the conventional perspectives.

- **Pull them together.** Gorillas are territorial, so this in itself has to be done in a way that makes them feel safe – and doesn't create an opportunity for any particularly ambitious gorilla to try to assert dominance.

- **Help them build a shared understanding of the community's deepest needs.** Gorillas are smart, but they know their own territory better than anything else. We need to help them see the whole picture through facts and through stories, and help them understand how their most urgent issues, their own piece of ground, relates to the health of the rest of the environment. And if we have included the gorillas who got left out in the past, they might have things to say that the more conventional gorillas don't want to hear. But they need to hear those perspectives, so sometimes we have to help them.

- **Lead them through the process of identifying priorities.** With so many gorillas and none of the old silverbacks left, consensus is crucial but seldom comes easily. Someone, perhaps you, has to lead -- but not the old way, with growling and chest-pounding and intimidation. They need to co-create those priorities, together. Your job may be to give them the process for doing that.

- **Don't leave getting it done to chance.** Gorillas can be powerful, but a lot of other issues are demanding their attention. The most successful communities not only make a plan, but set up the process for making it get done. One community that has an impressive history of successes in the face of tough challenges set up a committee of Council, consisting of electeds, staff administrators and key members of the community. Their job? Literally, hold the feet of the City and other agencies to the fire of doing the work that the community set out for itself through the plan. No shirking. We are watching, plan in hand.

Food for thought:

Who are your community's real gorillas today? Do they work together? How can you help them to work together on an important issue?

We no longer live in an era where we can take resilient, vibrant communities for granted (maybe we only thought we could). We have to work with the gorillas we have. And we can do that, but we have to consciously shift our methods to help that happen.

What does winning matter?

"How do we win?"

I hear economic development types ask that a lot. I heard the head of economic development for a large U.S. State talk at a conference about the state's ability to win... even after trumpeting the long-range investments the state had made in workforce development, in transitioning the state's economy. The key question he came back to: the state's ability to "win."

Win what?

"How do we win" is the wrong question.

Too often, we have thought that we "won" and the win turned out to be hollow. Or it came at the cost of unpleasant side effects.

And too often we have conveniently ignored the fact that someone, perhaps many someones, lost a lot so that we could "win."

Improving a place we care about is more complicated than a foot race. What does the model for economic development look like if we assume that the goal is something with more real meaning than "winning?"

If we allow the emphasis to remain on competing and "winning," without fully understanding what we are trying to win or why, then we may be trapped in an eternal deteriorating spiral without understanding why all our "winning" isn't making peoples' lives better.

Magic Bullets and Portfolios

I initially wrote this piece at a conference, listening to the keynote speaker from the back of the room. While feeling pretty discouraged, even though I definitely support the speaker's message: Locally-grown businesses are critical to local economies, and they should be a high priority for a community's economic development attention.

Amen, preach it, brother. Right there with you.

But then I started to get worried.

As much as I buy into the importance of small business — and there's a section coming up that's all about it — *thinking that we are going to revitalize or grow our local economies exclusively through this method means falling prey to the magic bullet myth.* The same myth that underlies urban renewal, convention center building, pedestrian malls and a whole host of other projects that were supposed to magically solve all our communities' problems.

If you build it, they will come.

The fact of the matter is that regional and national economies have changed since the days when our purchasing was limited by our walking distance. As consumers, we have a stunning array of choices, from local businesses to near-instant online emporiums -- places that we can buy from without even knowing where they are in the world. And if you expand your view beyond retail, which is of course only a small element of a local economy, the fact of the matter is that the economic universe has become simultaneously more fragmented and more interconnected. If I manufacture something, I can choose to make a highly specialized widget that I sell directly to companies anywhere in the world, or I can make a mass-produced doohickey to stock on the shelves at the mega-mart. I can do either, or both, from the same town and the same building.

My concern isn't with the message - like I said, it's an important message. My concern is with the one-note nature of the message — and more importantly, with many of the "here's how to fix your economy!!!" messages.

I just finished insisting that local economies are ecosystems, interconnected locally and interconnected with the world. Our local communities aren't sealed biospheres in a glass globe; they are at once their own creatures and part of the larger region, country and world.

> What problems could a one-shot approach generate? Oversupply? A cost-cutting race to the bottom? Vacant buildings designed for this economy and not suited for other uses?

Historically, when we have focused on a one-shot approach, we have done so without answering all the questions we should have answered, and that often creates bigger problems. Without knowing what demand a community can generate for local services, what problems could a one-shot approach generate? Oversupply? A cost-cutting race to the bottom? Vacant buildings designed for this small business economy and not suited for other uses?

We do need to focus our attention, and a large part of our focus should be on our locally-grown small business community. But we need to maintain more than one focus, because our communities have more than one dimension.

We need to build our communities' economies as *portfolios* -- we need to choose the best opportunities across a variety of sectors and strategies, and we need to spread our resources -- strategically, and not scattershot, but not put them all in one basket.

We have no magic bullets – not even the ones that we *want* to believe have those powers.

Food for Thought:

Is your community as a whole investing in lots of different areas of economic growth, or only a few?

If you don't know, you might check the public budget reports of key organizations.

Undercurrent #2:

Unintended Consequences

As communities — as humans, really — we do a consistently lousy job of remembering that our brilliant ideas and why- hasn't- anyone- else- thought- of- this- holy- shit- I'm-a-genius moments... have this annoying tendency to not turn out exactly the way we intended.

Sometimes our brilliant idea just plain doesn't work, but even more often it does *exactly* what we intended - and a whole lot more besides.

Those additional impacts are called unintended consequences. And psychologists and cognitive scientists have demonstrated that we are inclined to overestimate how much we know what we are doing. They've also documented that, unless we force ourselves to do otherwise, we tend to ignore the fact that our choices can create or set us up for other impacts that were not what we had in mind.

So welcome to Human Existence 101.

This is one of those situations where the mental tricks we evolved to help us survive the Ice Age don't fit so well with the complexities of our societies today. If you're a nomadic hunter-gatherer, thinking through all of the things that could go wrong with that mastodon hunt might mean that you starved in the cave.

The problem is that we live, of course, in much more complex environments now — and we have found in the last 150 years or so that we have to actively manage those environments. And we try to improve our communities using the same

> We place faith in our ability to find and implement The Right Answer, and allow ourselves to conveniently forget to think about what else might go wrong.

basic mental tools that allowed us to hunt mastodons. We place faith in our ability to find and implement The Right Answer, and allow ourselves to conveniently forget to think about what else might go wrong.

All that would be excusable, if it weren't for the fact that so much of our communities' current problems are themselves the unintended consequences of another generation's overconfident Right Answer.

Think about how these 20th and 21st-century innovations have impacted your community. They had benefits as intended, to be sure, but also created new, often wide-ranging problems:

- Urban Renewal
- Highway construction
- Exurban new housing construction
- Pension underfunding
- Culvertizing creeks
- Retail oversupply
- Teach to the test

You will probably have your own list of unintended impacts. For sake of reference, here's mine:

- More infrastructure than we have easily-available, non-painful-to-extract money to take care of.

- Regions that are too spread out to walk or serve with transit when we discover that our old assumptions about everyone driving a car don't work anymore (too many old people, gas got too expensive, etc.).

- Populations that were displaced from stable, if not

wealthy, neighborhoods, making a mess of social fabric and teaching generations that the systems that were supposed to help them were equally likely to screw them over.

- Buildings, parking lots, acres, more acres that don't have an economic use — at least, not an economic use that can pay for itself *and* pay for cleaning up the mess left by the thing that was there before.

- Government and nonprofit budgets under unrelenting, unending pressure to cut cut cut cut, while at the same time doing more more more more. If you work in governments and you feel the need to bludgeon the next person who says you should do "more with less," I can hold your books for you.

So much of what we face in communities today can be traced directly back to the Bright Ideas and Magic Bullet Solutions of previous generations. Huge amounts of the resources we have to work with have to be chewed up, sucked up by, consumed by undoing impacts that the Big Idea generators of past generations never thought of, or never admitted to thinking of back then.

So you'd think we would know better, that we'd put at least some thought into not getting fooled again.

But we don't.

Too often, we set ourselves up to make the same exact mistake. You can spot that coming when you hear a phrase like "We Just Have To..."

Implement a form-based code
Build a train system

Build a convention center/ball park/big something
Hire a Very Expensive Consultant

Spend a lot of money.

Unintended Consequences. They're real, they exist, and they aren't going away. So we have to learn to deal with them better.

And we can. There's no easy formula, but there are ways we can become more rigorous in thinking them through. The next few sections will talk about a few ways we can do that.

And because one of the characteristics that we commonly attribute to people who are Wise is the ability to think ahead, we'll frame a lot of this in terms of wise people. Think Einstein, Mandela, maybe your mom. My kids would probably not think of their mom.

> **Food for thought:**
>
> What's a Big Project that has happened in your community, and what were some of the unintended consequences of that?
>
> If you don't know from your own experience, you might want to look at a few old news articles or talk to some people who were impacted.
>
> Bonus points if you talk to people who were impacted and are from a different background from yourself.

Think of the story of the Wise Men in the Christian Bible. Three people recognize the signs in advance of what's going to happen, they react appropriately, and then they anticipate what could happen if they go back and tell the king where the baby is (OK, they had a little help with that last part, but go with it.) Their wise choice to go back home a different way avoided an unintended consequence.

Of course, it set up a <u>different, rather awful unintended consequence</u>. Which also tells us something.

Unintended consequences, sometimes bad ones, will still happen sometimes, despite our best efforts to anticipate and head them off. But that doesn't mean we don't have an obligation to try to prevent them.

Drifters and Destiny Commanders

We all allow some decisions to get made by default. Last week I could not decide whether it was worth my time to attend an event, and I was frankly relieved when I discovered that the deadline to register had passed. Circumstances made the decision for me. For little things with marginal benefits, the occasional decision- that- I-don't-have-to-make-because-life-made-it-for-me can be a welcome break from the constant load of responsibility.

But what happens to us when we don't make an important decision? What happens to most people who drift through their careers or their relationships without making conscious choices about where to invest their time, or which responsibilities to put first?

> When it comes to managing and governing our communities, we allow circumstances to make decisions for us more often than any of us want to admit.

Most of us know, at least intellectually, that there are important points in our lives where we have to make a conscious choice, and where if we don't make a conscious choice, chances are we will regret it later.

But when it comes to managing and governing our communities, we allow circumstances to make decisions for us more often than any of us want to admit.

The community leadership doesn't come to agreement over whether a proposed development is a good idea (probably because there is no shared vision of what our community should be). And often the people who have the job of making that decision secretly hope that the

73

developer will just give up, because then it will be Not My Fault.

Or we as citizens know that our community is facing some big issues down the road – aging populations, aging buildings, aging roads – and we know in our guts that if we don't do something, we will be in deep trouble sooner or later. But the tradeoffs are unpleasant, we don't easily agree on what we need to do, we have to find the money to do whatever needs to be done. Too many times, we let it go... until Next Year, Next Budget, Next Administration.

Which easily turns into the Next and the Next and the Next.

Not deciding benefits us short-term because it makes today easier, and it keeps us from having to change the way we do things today. And who knows, maybe some sugar daddy will come along while we are procrastinating and solve it all for us. But probably not.

In failing to act, we abdicate the opportunity to take control of our future – to do what is in our power to position our communities for future success. We also lose the opportunity to define for ourselves how our community should be, rather than letting the winds of fate blow us into something we didn't want.

A few communities take this initiative, but too many communities drift through their big decisions – at least until drifting, not thinking ahead and not anticipating unintended consequences lands the community in a crisis.

Here is the deep challenge, though: we cannot assume that we can just snap our fingers and transform our communities from drifters into Destiny Commanders. As I said to clients *ad nauseum* over the years, if it were easy, you would have done it already.

We (and I) often speak of communities as though they were individuals, and as though a "community" had one completely shared set of goals and objectives. We all know that's not really the case. Because communities are complex, and in most cases more complex today than ever, our ability to develop a community-wide shared vision of the future and a shared understanding of the community's needs and priorities has far outstripped our intuitive or common sense ability to do that.

When we had much smaller and simpler communities – and when we only cared what a tiny fraction of the community's residents thought – it was a relatively easy proposition to make democratic, or at least supposedly democratic, decisions. That's why we have public deliberation processes based on the ideal of the classical debate: if everyone who has a seat at the table shares the same fundamental perspective, then you have a shared base of understanding and mutual respect that enables rational debate and evaluation of potential alternatives. If you are all fundamentally the same, then you have a shared language to work from.

You don't have to watch CNN, or your local cable broadcast of a public hearing, for very long to see that this isn't the case anymore. People who come to the podium, or write the letters, or protest on the street, come from

When we had much smaller and simpler communities –

and when we only cared what a tiny fraction of the community's residents thought –

it was a relatively easy proposition to make democratic, or at least supposedly democratic, decisions.

75

more fundamentally different backgrounds, perspectives, and priorities than we have ever had before. Obviously that's essential and necessary – a government that only listens to a quarter or less of its residents is no democracy at all.

But regardless of your spot on the political spectrum, it's clear that this process isn't working well, either at many local levels or higher up the chain. And this dysfunctionality leaves us drifting. It robs us of the capacity we need to make the important decisions, and it does so at a time when the decisions are probably as critical as they have been in generations.

———

The aggravating piece is that we can most definitely find ways to fix this. Larger businesses with diverse workforces figured out more than 20 years ago that they could not simply rely on common sense assumptions and whatever social skills people learned in elementary school to enable them to do the increasingly complex work that the companies needed. If you are in a cutting-edge car factory or a leading pharmaceutical firm today, managers and staff receive training in specific, step-by-step methods for enabling constructive conversations, managing teams of diverse people, setting priorities and making group decisions.

Larger businesses with diverse workforces figured out more than 20 years ago that they could not simply rely on common sense assumptions and whatever social skills people learned in elementary school to enable them to do the increasingly complex work that the companies needed.

Debates happen, disagreements occur, some people do better than others, but the overall process is designed to make complex decisions involving a large number of people and move the company's objectives forward. And it's not rocket science -- an hour grazing on www.hbr.com will give you a good taste of how this generally works.

But why has so little of what the academic and business worlds can tell us about effective decision-making has found its way into our government and community decision-making processes?

It's no wonder that so many communities are drifting. We are using 19th century tools to deal with a 21st century world, hanging onto our wooden mallet when the nail gun is sitting in an open box across the room. With the complexity and increasing urgency of the big challenges facing our communities today, we have to start using the tools that will help us make the conscious decisions we need to build our communities' futures.

Food for Thought:

Think about two different multi-person experiences you have had lately. Maybe a board meeting and a public hearing, or a lunch and a presentation about a proposed project in your neighborhood.

List the unwritten rules of interaction that governed both events (such as, you will sit in these chairs, you can or cannot interrupt if someone makes a mistake, etc.)

Imagine what would happen if the unwritten rules were different, or if you switched the rules between the two events.

Multiple Futures, or Find Your Shoes Before Mom Gets an Ulcer

I have two sons, and when the younger one was 9, I wrote this about him (I have to put in that caveat because now he's 18 and actually outgrew at least this part of his life's disorganization. More on him later).

Every weekday morning he goes to school. To go to school, he has to put on his shoes. How often during a week do you think he does that without my telling him to find his shoes before he misses the bus? How often do you think he says to himself, "OK, bus time in five minutes, I'd better go get my shoes."

The answer is: not often. He's not thinking ahead, and if he waits until the last second and can't find his shoes, he has a problem. If he thought ahead past the second he is living in, he would save himself (and Mom) a lot of aggravation.

For my son, considering the possibility that his shoes might not be where he thinks they are would (I hope) change his behavior – he would leave himself a little bit more time to find them in case they are under his bed or on a shelf if the closet (why??) instead of by the door. He would anticipate other possibilities than the one that's supposed to happen.

That wouldn't mean that he would have to account for every remotely conceivable possibility -- the chance that an alligator breaks into our house in Ohio and eats his shoes is about .0001%, so it wouldn't make sense for him to build an alligator trap in the hydrangeas to make sure that he can get his shoes on.

Thinking ahead would mean, however, that he would identify a few possible issues that could get in the way of his goal of getting on the bus on time, and allocate some of his resources (in his case, his time) to making sure that he has anticipated and planned for the most likely potential factors that could get in the way of his goal.

—

We often fail to think ahead about the choices we make as communities. If we build that new road, or stick all our money in that grant, or allow that neighborhood to deteriorate, what do we think will happen?

What else could happen?

And what else?

How likely are those impacts?

How will that decision and its potential impacts change the world around it, and how might those changes force other decisions in the future?

—

What we usually do when we try to figure out the future: we create a linear extrapolation. We look at where we are and where we've been, and we draw a straight line through those points, charging out into the future, straight as an arrow. Something like this:

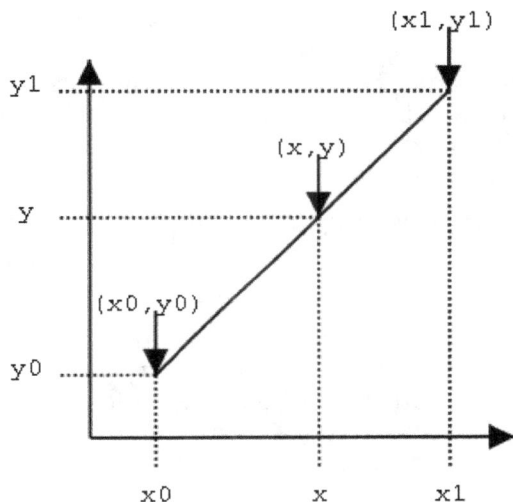

There are two fundamentals at work here:

- First, we base our assumptions on the idea that all of the factors that defined our past will continue to define our future. We extrapolate the future from the past.

- Second: we assume that our extrapolation will allow us to predict a single future outcome—that straight line implies that there is, fundamentally, only one logical outcome that can derive from those extrapolated conditions.

We might look at a bunch of factors, we might create a variety of extrapolations, but we usually average that variety out. And we end up with one straight or neatly arcing line.

That's great, because it gives us a nice, easy, concrete,

manageable future. We will need 3,424 additional housing units, we will be able to support 150,000 additional square feet of retail space, we will see an increase in traffic on Road X of 350%, which obviously means we have to build a new road or make a superhighway out of that thing. Isn't that good to know?

Only two root problems with linear extrapolations:

- First, that easy number turns out to be often, and often wildly, wrong.

- Second, the easy number can too easily become a self-fulfilling prophecy. If we "know" what the future will hold, we build for that, and we might make it happen. Unintended and unwanted consequences and all.

Interestingly, the most successful businesses don't use straight linear extrapolations anymore – they outgrew that somewhere in the last 20 years. Instead, the current state of the art is to identify multiple potential future situations, and then plan for the key drivers of and prevailing needs created by those future situations. So instead of the simple straight line, you get something more like this:

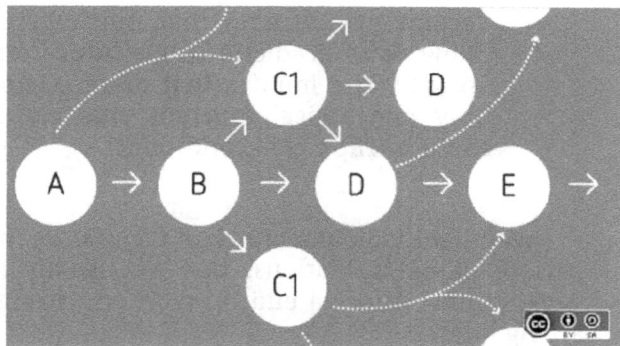

From p2plab.gr, subject to Creative Commons license.

The dots represent different future situations, and the arrows represent the most likely future possibilities. Not quite as simple, but a lot more insightful if we want to create strategies that will help us find success in a future that we have to honestly admit that we cannot predict.

If, as communities, we thought through the potential impacts of the choices we made in the past, we would have probably anticipated at least some of the issues that we face in local economies today. We might have anticipated that demolishing urban neighborhoods to build highways could destabilize entire populations, and we might have guessed that new building upstream might result in increased flooding downstream. We probably couldn't have predicted everything, but we could have probably headed off a few of them.

Instead, we have largely noted these impacts with surprise after they occur.

> Instead of thinking of the future as a straight line that takes our current trends and projects them growing predictably into the future, we have to start thinking about multiple potential futures.

We might have had an excuse for being overly simplistic and assuming straight extrapolations in the mid-20th century, when many of our tools and ideas for where we lived and how we got around were new, and we were more naïve about what might happen. But we don't have that excuse anymore. If a simple straight-line prediction of items such as population growth, market demand, or traffic generation ever made any sense, it certainly doesn't now.

Instead of thinking of the future as a straight line that takes our current trends and projects them growing predictably into the future, we have to start thinking about multiple potential futures. We need to evaluate what happens if the projections come in much lower, or much higher, than current trends would indicate. If we miss the mark too broadly, we may not have the resources to deal with the impacts of our mistakes. A wise approach to evaluating future likelihoods would look at the range of possible trajectories, select a manageable number that seem most likely, and design the plan to address those. And of course, revise the assumptions frequently.

Food for Thought:

Identify a specific decision that you, your organization or your local government made, preferably one that was made more than five years ago.

Identify how that decision has played out, and three to five critical factors that led to it happening that way. These might be things that someone else did, or they might be things out of anyone's control.

In your imagination, change one of those factors, and think through how that might have changed the outcome. Would other people have responded differently? Would a different outcome have become possible… or possible?

Externalities R Us

A wise person doesn't only think ahead, he or she also anticipates and prepares to deal proactively with the unintended consequences of a decision.

That sounds like an oxymoron – how do you anticipate your unintended consequences?

This is why thinking ahead becomes so important -- if we think rigorously and systematically about the things we decide to do, we can often anticipate that there are possible consequences to our decisions that we didn't intend.

———

The easiest unintended consequences to figure out are those that will impact me directly – the ones that will come back to bite me in the butt. If I am thinking about putting an addition on my house that I really can't afford, and doing so will put me at risk of being unable to pay all my other bills, then the potential unintended consequences of my choice to add onto my house are pretty obvious. Since I will have to deal personally with those unintended consequences, they are part of my system. That means that these consequences should be relatively easy to see, if I am honest with myself about what all might happen. I might delude myself into thinking I can have it all, but that's not failing to think ahead. That's just being a dumbass.

The hardest, and potentially most troubling, types of unintended consequences fall into

> The hardest, and potentially most troubling, types of unintended consequences fall into a group that traditional invisible-hand economics call "externalities."

a group that traditional invisible-hand economics call "externalities." Externalities are the impacts of a decision that accrue to someone or something else -- the impacts are external to the person or organization that made the decision.

Traditional economic theory placed externalities outside of the economy – the externality was experienced by someone other than the economic actors, so it was not part of the economic activity. Terming something an "externality" was a way to exclude it from the equation.

Of course, it's not that simple.

As I mentioned, my father and grandfather ran a small paint company in the 1960s and 1970s. In those days, there were few rules regulating hazardous materials, and most of the compounds in paint hadn't been officially recognized as hazardous anyways. Like most paint factories, theirs generated lots of garbage – batches of paint that didn't come out right, test pots, empty containers, broken equipment, etc.

The company was located on the edge of a steep gorge that ran through town ... and standard operating procedure at the factory was to toss the cans, pots and other garbage over the hillside. This wasn't uncommon – people used to use that gorge to discard a lot of types of refuse. I remember 1950s-era car fenders and mattresses in the brush along the hillside farther downriver.

The company closed in the early 1980s, and as far as I know all of the officers and stockholders are dead. But the old paint cans on the side of the gorge are probably still leaking – my brothers, who still live in the area, have heard friends talk about seeing rainbow-colored scum on the creek surface downstream from the factory site.

When the day comes when that property gets cleaned up, it won't be my dad's company doing it. Instead, it will probably be the state Environmental Protection Agency. Which means that, even though I didn't do the polluting, as a taxpayer, I and all of my neighbors across the state will pick up the tab.

The problem with most externalities, from a local economy point of view, is that those impacts aren't really external to us at all. One way or another, they end up affecting us as individuals, and us as a community. Most of the time it falls to a public agency, like the EPA, to go on the front line of dealing with externalities, whether it's environmental cleanup or sheltering people who cannot survive in the modern economy on their own. And if no one deals with the externality, it will create its own set of consequences and impacts to us or to others, who will in turn impact us. And as we continuously challenge our local governments and state agencies to deal with more and more externalities with less and less resources, our capacity to manage unexpected consequences continues to erode.

> The problem with most externalities, from a local economy point of view, is that those impacts aren't really external to us at all. One way or another, they end up affecting us as individuals, and us as a community.

At the end of the day, all of this means that the externality isn't external to us as a community at all. There really are no externalities, because none of us live in isolation, entirely separated from the impacts created by others. There is actually little or nothing that can be excluded from the economic equation – we live in a complex, interdependent system, not Adam Smith's series of simple, separate transactions.

There isn't an easy answer, or a magic hat consultant,

or a download-from-the-app-store solution. Our only choice: use the best thinking and decision-making tools we can come up with to try to systematically avoid or manage externalities. We can work to identify the potential unintended consequences of decisions, we can use the tools available to prevent or manage externalities, and we can keep a close eye out for new unanticipated consequences that we will have to address.

Because we will have to address them. It's just a matter of time.

Food for Thought:

Think about an decision that your organization, local government or agency made recently. Write down the key points of the decision.

For each of the key points, identify a potential externality. How could that decision impact others -- for good or for bad?

Try to figure out whether the externalities you identified were addressed in the preparation for the decision.

Evaluate, Already

Storm Cunningham, author of <u>ReWealth</u> and other books, pointed out to me one time that communities seldom do any forensic work on their past plans and economic development strategies, so the whole process lacks the kind of feedback that other industries have. And that leads to exactly the same behavior--and quality standards--decade after decade.

> [We] desperately need to have after-action reports (like the military) analyzing what went wrong and right. But neither the public client nor the private provider are interested in seeing their failures exposed, so the industry languishes in "going through the motions" mode.[1]

Other than anecdotes and our gut sense, we often don't really know whether a particular recommendation for pir community was a good idea or a bad idea, even years later. We cannot really say whether our ideas or programs had the intended effect or unintended consequences. We know from the experience of the last few decades that big ideas can go badly awry, but we don't fully know when or why that might have happened.

There is not much reason to trust a situation where we praise the process and the product, but have no idea what the results will be.

Of course, there's three very practical reasons why that evaluation doesn't happen:

1. **No one likes to see their mistakes exposed.** Much easier to move on, to leave it in the past.

---

[1] Personal email exchange, 2012.

2. Local and regional governments and community nonprofits — and their staff — are **generally hard pressed to get through the day-to-day requirements** they have to meet to keep the place running. Going back through the records and teasing out how the plan did or didn't influence development or decisions usually looks like decadent luxury.

3. **A lot of time has to pass** -- probably at least 5 to 10 years -- before the recommendations of any kind of moderately ambitious plan substantially play out. Which means that there may be no one left who remembers the plan to begin with, and if they do, they are probably ready to move on to the next iteration and not mess around with the old one.

All of which makes me think that evaluating the effectiveness of long-range plans and economic development strategies might be one of the most influential activities that university programs could undertake. If academics and students devoted at least a portion of their time to understanding how past plans did and didn't work, instead of focusing exclusively on how they *ought to* work, they would not only fill in some glaring holes in our theories and practices, but the students would come out of school with a more rounded understanding of what our usual methods can - and do, and do *not* - do. That would make them better professionals, and it would make them

> Evaluating the effectiveness of long-range plans and economic development strategies might be one of the most influential activities that university programs could undertake.

more effective professionals. And the insight that they helped create would equip us with a higher capability to actually make something happen.

Design Arrogance and the Lesson of America

A few years ago, an interview with one of the current luminaries of the New Urbanist movement was published in which the august personage asserted that public participation requirements are too onerous to enable great design work to be done. The ignorant NIMBY rabble kept getting in the way.

Early in my career I worked as a public historian and historic preservation specialist, so rather than launch immediately into my opinion, let me tell you a true story.

In the 1950s, business owners in downtowns across the country became agitated over the fact that their central business districts were facing a double challenge: increasing amounts of traffic congestion and increasing competition from new suburban shopping centers. One of the cities that faced this was Green Bay, Wisconsin, which had a very energetic and forward-thinking business leadership circle. I knew many of those leaders years later, when I had responsibility for dealing with some of the unintended consequences and externalities of their decisions.

The good men of Green Bay did what most forward-thinking leaders do when faced with a fearful challenge on the horizon: they hired a consultant. The consultant they chose was Victor Gruen, an architect who had recently gained fame designing the nation's first enclosed shopping mall, in Edina, Minnesota. In the couple of years that had lapsed since the Southland Mall plans hit the streets, Gruen had become a celebrity – the Andreas Duany of his day.

In a 2004 article for the New Yorker, Malcolm Gladwell described Gruen as "short, stout, and unstoppable, with a wild head of hair and eyebrows like unpruned hedgerows." Gladwell summed up Gruen's impact on that era, and today, pretty succinctly:

> Victor Gruen didn't design a building; he designed an archetype. For a decade, he gave speeches about it and wrote books and met with one developer after another and waved his hands in the air excitedly, and over the past half century that archetype has been reproduced so faithfully on so many thousands of occasions that today virtually every suburban American goes shopping or wanders around or hangs out in a Southdale facsimile at least once or twice a month. Victor Gruen may well have been the most influential architect of the twentieth century. He invented the mall.[2]

Gruen insisted in Green Bay, as he did in dozens of other cities in the 1950s and 1960s, that the key to solving downtown's problems was to completely separate vehicular traffic from pedestrians. By massively widening Main Street at the north end of the commercial district, and completely enclosing the core of the existing commercial district, all of downtown's problems would be solved. All it required was money and a willingness to be unsentimental and practical.

You don't have to be Gladwell to understand what happened. It took 20 years for Gruen's vision to obtain some form of reality, and during that time the City's business and political leadership, and its planning staff, stuck to Gruen's plan as diligently as the real world constraints of financing and private development would enable. Of course, those real world constraints enabled it a lot less than Gruen envisioned.

By the time it opened in 1977, the new Port Plaza Mall

---

[2] Malcolm Gladwell, "The Terrazzo Jungle." *The New Yorker,* http://www.newyorker.com/archive/2004/03/15/040315fa_fact1

and associated parking lots and garages had obliterated acres of downtown buildings, dislocated a hundred residents, and sent dozens of businesses to liquidation or the far edges of the newly-sprawling city, where many of them remain today.

The collateral damage of grand ideas. If Gruen thought of them at all, I wager he simply thought that was the price of progress.

All of this might be OK, at least from a strict economic standpoint, if Gruen's grand plan had worked.

It didn't.

Port Plaza Mall lost money from virtually Day 1. By the early 1980s, Port Plaza was doing so poorly that the City took the advice of another consultant and bulldozed another full block of buildings to add the magic third anchor, which they were assured was the way to fix the mall's problems. By the early 2000s, that anchor was gone.

Green Bay, like many other cities that drank the downtown mall Kool-Aid, continued for years to struggle with a downtown dominated by a windowless, dispiriting, too-much-vacant hulk where its heart should be. Meanwhile, the region's former skid row, right across the Fox River within eyesight of the mall, became the hottest urban neighborhood in the region, and the winner of a Great American Main Street Award in 2009.

———

This isn't a story about the virtues of historic preservation, although the Green Bay story is certainly a good object lesson for the old Kenneth Galbraith quotation.[3]

> Gruen's mall failed because he envisioned and sold an ideal solution without giving attention to economic realities, and without consideration of the myriad of unforeseen factors and unintended consequences that could, and did, develop.

Gruen's idea didn't fail because Green Bay wanted old buildings, or because the people who lived and worked in those old downtown buildings did something to undermine the plan. Like most people of that era, the majority of the City's leadership and residents placed their faith in the expert and in the idea of progress. What gut misgivings they may have had were pushed aside. The plan was made by an expert, a national expert, right?

Gruen's mall failed because he envisioned and sold an ideal solution without giving attention to economic realities, and without consideration of the myriad of unforeseen factors and unintended consequences that could, and did, develop. It's possible to say that Gruen could have tried to understand development economics, but even if he did, fully anticipating those unforeseen factors would have been impossible. Gruen stood at the beginning of an era, and there was no way anyone could anticipate how the world would change in a few short decades.

---

[3] "The preservation movement has one great curiosity. There is never retrospective controversy or regret. Preservationists are the only people in the world who are invariably confirmed in their wisdom after the fact." Quoted in *Measuring the Economics of Preservation: Recent Findings* by Place Economics, June 2011. http://www.achp.gov/docs/final-popular-report6-7-11.pdf

The greatest failure of Gruen's plan was that he did not recognize or acknowledge that his Grand Vision could very well turn out all wrong.

—

We should have learned by now that our Grand Visionary Designers are not infallible. Our landscapes are littered with Grand Visionary Architecture that was supposed to fix something, or create Something Big. And so few of those grand visions ever came out the way they were promised, or managed not to create a new set of problems. Never heard of Port Plaza? That's because there are Port Plazas of one flavor or another in virtually every city in the country. Some are malls, some are stadiums, some are brutalistic, forsaken parks. You can pick them out easily by their Grand Design ambitions and their total lack of life.

> Understanding the real reasons why people oppose a project requires the willingness to do so, the humility to listen, and the internal fortitude and self-assurance to admit that possibly, oh just possibly, we don't know everything that there is to know.

The fact that we haven't learned this lesson is a blot on architecture, and planning. And economic governance. And community leadership, writ large.

Understanding the real reasons why people oppose a project requires the willingness to do so, the humility to listen, and the internal fortitude and self-assurance to admit that possibly, oh just possibly, we don't know everything that there is to know. That is the real mark of wisdom.

—

Marquee designer types have the privilege of maintaining a distance from the dirty work of making a project functional in real life. I have worked with many of the nameless landscape architects and architects who are hired by the developers after the Grand Visionary types are paid, have gathered their glory and big checks and left. And it is those highly competent, highly talented professionals who deal with the fact that the Grand Architect ignored the steep slope under that proposed building, or face the fact that the charming landscaped driveway empties out onto a major intersection and those planting beds will block other drivers' ability to see cars pulling out.

How much of that could the marquee designers have learned, and anticipated, and fixed, by simply listening with honesty and humility to the people who are experts in that specific location?

How much would Gruen have learned about how the community's businesses would or would not fit into his Grand Design?

Ah, little stuff. Who cares?

If the people who live around a proposed development oppose that development, chances are they know something that is important to the health of their neighborhood, and the larger community as well. If we think that we are too much hot stuff to have to listen to them, then we are no better than little Napoleons in big capes, creating monuments to our hubris that our children and grandchildren will have to clean up.

And in fact, we will be worse than that, because the object lessons of the damage we can do in our ignorance already exist all around us.

—

Gladwell describes the end of Gruen's life in terms that remind me of a Greek myth:

> The lesson of America was that the grandest of visions could be derailed by the most banal of details, like the size of the retail footprint, or whether Congress set the depreciation allowance at forty years or twenty years.
>
> When, late in life, Gruen came to realize this, it was a powerfully disillusioning experience. He revisited one of his old shopping centers... and pronounced himself in "severe emotional shock." Developers were interested only in profit. "I refuse to pay alimony for those bastard developments," he said in a speech in London, in 1978.
>
> He turned away from his adopted country. He had fixed up a country house outside of Vienna, and soon he moved back home for good. But what did he find when he got there? Just south of old Vienna, a mall had been built—in his anguished words, a "gigantic shopping machine." It was putting the beloved independent shopkeepers of Vienna out of business. It was crushing the life of his city. He was devastated. Victor Gruen invented the shopping mall in order to make America more like Vienna. He ended up making Vienna more like America.[4]

4

http://www.newyorker.com/archive/2004/03/15/040315fa_fact1#ixzz1C4d

Undercurrent #3:

Talent: Not what we thought it was. Much more.

This section has changed the most since 2013. In the first edition of this book, I highlighted the growing importance of Talent -- high-skill employees in high-demand fields -- as an economic development tool. In 2013, I wrote a lot about being authentic and presenting your community to potential Talent the way you actually are, and I also added some uncomfortable stuff about whether that Talent wants what we have to offer.

And most uncomfortably, I tried - and failed - to explore what we do about the people in our community who aren't Talent. As I wrote in the essay "We have Animals More Equal Than Others," *some Talent is more Equal than others*. Which is, if you accept democratic principles, very unsettling.

I could see the conflict, but I didn't have an answer to that problem.

Because I had gotten stuck in the standard paradigm as well.

The mistake that I made in 2013,and that others across the country have made since: that Talent is super picky, capricious, and rare. Screamingly rare. Just under unicorn-level rare. And because those near-unicorns *are* so rare, we have to do whatever we can to give *them* what they want, brush ourselves up to *their* levels, fit ourselves to *them* like a fine suit.

Sure, we shouldn't try to sell our community as an XXL if we were actually a Medium, but the basic point was the same: "sell" our community to the people most likely to buy it.

> But Talent isn't rare. Perfect, ready-made, use-right-out-of-the-box Talent is somewhat rare. But even today, our communities are chock full of Talent.

Talent wasn't really comparable to the coal and steel that provided the raw materials for the Industrial Era, which was the surface analogy people like me kept using. This Talent was more like precious metals, super hard to access and maintain and requiring this constant, anxious investment in keeping them from being poached away by someone offering a little bit more.

But Talent isn't rare. Perfect, ready-made, use-right-out-of-the-box Talent is somewhat rare. But even today, our communities are chock full of Talent.

Our Talent doesn't always look or sound or act like 2013 Della thought it should. And sometimes it needs some polish, some investment, that we have been stupidly resistant to making.

> Our organization systems (business and government) still look, under their fancy covers, more like a 1900s whip factory than anything that fits a Fusion Era.

But the bigger problem is this: our organization systems (business and government) still look, under their fancy covers, more like a 1900s whip factory than anything that fits a Fusion Era. And in many respects, this Talent looks more Fusion Era than the organizations understand or assume.

So our Talent and our systems, once again, are living in different, conflicting paradigms. So it's not surprising that the near-unicorns are hard to hold, and the Talent-in-the-making regards our invitations with suspicion. Our biggest Talent pools, after all, are the people who have been burned by us before.

———

I made a point in an earlier chapter, and in about everything I've written in the last 5 years, about how diverse teams working within an empowering structure create more innovative work than conventional approaches. That was the foundation for one of the businesses I cofounded post-2013, and it achieved some pretty impressively innovative results.

But when you try to put diverse groups of people into the same old systems that you used for the plain-vanilla homogenous groups, three things go wrong:

1. **Talent that doesn't fit the old molds will get kicked out of the conventional systems,** unless there is a conscious effort made to adapt the old system to these new opportunities. It's way easier for the gatekeepers of The Way We Do Things to reject this new Talent because it doesn't look right or sound right or have the right degree, than it is to change their own paradigm to make room for new Talent.

2. Because most of those old systems were designed around people with shared backgrounds and shared basic assumptions (remember my description of 19th-century public meetings designed by and for white men), these systems don't have any way to **help people learn to navigate deep-rooted cultural differences** and age-old suspicions. And since pretty much nothing else in our lives does that, either, your diverse Talent can end up misunderstanding and mistrusting each other.

3. Our new Talent's profile of skills may not actually fit our systems -- not because of their education or diction, but because **they are ready to live in the Fusion Era, and we're still stuck in the Industrial Era.** We might be making something super high tech, or we're telling our employees or residents that we want them to "Innovate!!," but when they hit our conventional management or approval process, they learn in a hurry that what we said we wanted is not what our systems are telling them we wanted. Which throws a lot of doubt on our original claims of wanting them to innovate at all.

—

If true out-of-the-box, near-perfect Talent is also near-unicorn rare, it doesn't make much sense to make the whole effort about chasing them. Exotic trophy hunting isn't the best way for most of us to feed the household. And yet, this is exactly what a lot of conventional economic development efforts do.

Instead, the real challenge ahead of us is to help our own nascent Talent, with its unconventional approaches and its rough edges, to help the rest of us move into a resilient future.

Instead, the real challenge ahead of us is to help our own nascent Talent, with its unconventional approaches and its rough edges, to help the rest of us move into a resilient future.

This Undercurrent will include two things, which might not seem to fit together at first glance, but ultimately do:

- **The value of being true to what makes your place unique and authentic.** That still rings true, not only because of the potential to attract ready-made Talent, but because we need to retain and nurture our own Talent as well. And if we are refocusing on building up our native Talent, including the Talent we've overlooked in the past, we have to tell the truth more than ever. Not only will our own Talent spot our hypocrisies and overblown statements faster than anyone, but they want to be proud of their community, too.

- More on this question of **the mismatch between what we think Talent is supposed to be, and the actual Talent already living among us.** For that theme, I have adapted some elements from my most recent book, *Everybody Innovates Here*, because I think I said it in that book as well as I'm ever going to say it. So if you like those, you know where to look.

—

In her 2020 daily series of social media posts, historian Heather Cox Richardson did a stunning and timely job of drawing out a core conflict underlying the development of American democracy. As she frames it, a segment of the Founding Fathers believed that citizens could and should be fully entrusted to make their own decisions (their definition of a citizen left a lot to be desired, but it was a step forward in Western thinking at that time).

Other early American leaders believed that the majority of people could not be trusted to make sound decisions, and that they should function as the "mudsills" of society, obediently doing the work while their Betters made the decisions ("Mudsills" were not only Black slaves, but lower class people of all backgrounds).

As Dr. Richardson teases it out, most of the political conflicts of the last 200 years or more revolve around the fundamental conflict between these paradigms, as the supposed Mudsills fight for expanded rights, and the holders of the Mudsill belief push back.

> It appears that we have been speaking idealistically about our communities' Talent in one paradigm, but assuming that they are Mudsills in the other.

In the immediate aftermath of the 2020 elections, this core conflict of paradigms comes into particularly sharp relief. We can't avoid seeing that a large amount of the general populace still believes that elites should run the show, and Mudsills should be quiet and do the work. As that election has demonstrated, the democratic, people-have-potential paradigm cannot be taken for granted. And the "Mudsill" paradigm still has proponents, even though many of us may see that belief system, stripped of its decorations, as morally reprehensible.

It appears that we have been speaking idealistically about our communities' Talent in one paradigm, but assuming that they are Mudsills in the other.

Here's the nail that needs to go into the coffin of the Mudsill elitist model: we cannot afford, in unambiguous dollars and cents, to assume that our communities are mostly made up of Mudsills.

In a future where economic prosperity and problem-solving depends on human innovation and creativity, we will not survive on only a few fragile near-Unicorns. No amount of obedient Mudsills will enable us to create the innovations, the transformations, that our survival requires. It's like a city that depends on a nearly-dried-out reservoir, where only a smattering of rain replaces the thousands of gallons pulled out every year. After a certain point, no amount of promotions or magic or suit-fitting to those few privileged Talents will be able to do enough.

> In a future where economic prosperity and problem-solving depends on human innovation and creativity, we will not survive on only a few fragile near-Unicorns.

Instead, we need to build, enhance and retain our Talent. And re-design how we work to better fit them. And our shared future.

That which makes you unique makes you valuable

My biggest difficulty in Christmas shopping (other than trying to remember which Lego set the younger kid said was the really wonderful one, and which one was lame), is trying to find something that will be unique and valuable for the person who will get it. To be sure, I don't strive for that for everyone -- the gift for Great Aunt Sophie doesn't always get the same level of thought as others -- but to the extent that I can, for the people who really matter to me, I am looking for something that is

- different from what they will get from anyone else,
- different from what they already have, and
- something that they will value.

So for my cool sister-in-law, I am looking for a funky necklace made out of natural materials. For my niece, I am looking for an outfit that captures her free spirit and will look great on her. For my kids... well, you know, we get a list, most of which is incomprehensible to me anyways. Nevermind.

But here's the kicker: *I will probably be willing to pay at least a little bit more* for the perfect funky necklace or free-spirit outfit than I would for a typical string of beads or a boring t-shirt and pants. And because that's what I am looking for, I am also more likely to stray from the beaten path and go shopping somewhere other than Target.

The germ of the thought is this: *That which makes a place unique makes it more valuable to the people who want it.* And since we harp constantly on the need to win and retain Talent anymore, becoming valuable to at least some subset of that Talent matters more than ever. Talent will typically value your community more, care about it more, invest in it more, if the experience you offer differs in a valuable way from what they can get somewhere else.

A lot of times it's easy to see our communities as commodities, like the plastic toys on a shelf in a big store. If I can get the same transforming thingamabob at Big Box A vs. Big Box B, then I will probably buy it where it's cheapest. That's the general retail Race to the Bottom -- if there is nothing that makes your store different other than price, then you will win or lose based on how cheap you are. Any other factors go out the window.

> A lot of times it's easy to see our communities as commodities, like the plastic toys on a shelf in a big store.

But if you are the only store that carries the way cool thingamabob, then you not only win the sale, but you don't have to charge the rock-bottom price, right?

It's the same with our communities. If we regard them - and promote them - as commodities, then the only way that we attract new businesses or people (or keep the people and businesses that have the wherewithal to go elsewhere) is if we make ourselves the *lowest-price option.* That is what economic development incentives were about in the first place - making the costs of a location lower, or at least even with, the competition.

Think about it: If my community sales pitch is that " we are within 600 miles of 75% of the United States," and hundreds of other communities can make the same claim, then what reason does any Talented entrepreneur or business operator have to come to my community - unless I am the cheapest?

And when I am no longer the cheapest, what reason do they have to stay?

When it comes to creating a Wise Economy, our communities' ability to succeed long-term depends on our ability to capitalize on and communicate those features that make our community unique, and therefore valuable.

Food for Thought:

Do your neighbors actually believe that your community is special?

What *is* legitimately unique about it?

———

There are a lot of elements of any community that are nice but numbingly common - "we have a great work ethic," "we have rail service," etc.   But it's the unique elements - the ones that make your community different, the ones that cannot be replicated by someone else - that will make you more valuable to someone than anything incentive you can offer. If you are not playing to your uniqueness, then you are joining the Grand Caravan of Commodities on the Race to the Bottom.

A couple of important words of warning, though.

- First, **what is unique and valuable to one person is a white elephant to another**. If you establish yourself as something unique, you become like a gourmet cheese -- people will either pay more for your one-of-a-kind taste and texture, or they will drop you back on the shelf when they get a whiff of you.   If your downtown is renowned as the Victorian Antiques Capital of Your State, a lot of people would consider that a point in favor of moving there. I myself, on the other hand, will probably look somewhere else

- Second, **fake uniqueness will hurt you worse in the long run than being a commodity.** The Talent is on to you, whether you're recruiting them or trying to retain them. They can sniff out your fakery miles away.

- Third, remember that your community has many aspects that make it unique, and **it is that entire package, not just one Claim to Fame, that Talent will care about.** And different elements will appeal to different Talent groups. And that's a good thing. Relying on one Talent group would be like relying on one industry. Not the most prudent idea.

We have animals more equal than others...or do we?

All animals are equal, but some animals are more equal than others.

-George Orwell, *Animal Farm.*

That might be the most uncomfortable quote people remember from high school English. I suspect you at least sort of recall <u>the story:</u> barnyard animals, attempting to create an egalitarian society, end up with a pig-driven dictatorship.

<u>Paul Davidoff</u> does not approve.

Democracy 101 is pretty adamant on this point: everyone participates, everyone has a stake, if you're going to bend over backward for anyone, it had better be those who have historically not been given the same advantages – the poor, the less-educated, the minority. Everything is open, every voice has the same weight.

But we have a problem.

We live in a world where the economic potential, economic growth and long-term economic vibrancy of a community – really, its ability to stay alive – depends more and more on that place's supply of talented, creative, innovative people. From academics to local staffers, local economy discussions return over and over and over again to the same refrains:

We aren't attracting enough talent. How do we get more talent? Where do we find more talent? How do we keep talent here?

There is not a shortage of humans. There is apparently a shortage of talent. Which means there is a shortage of economic fuel, of the stuff that will determine whether we can pay for what we need or not.

We have a problem.

Our democratic principles say that all people are important, but the economic developers and the pragmatists say that only some of them are keeping us afloat. We feel obligated to say that everyone matters, but the cold hard fact is that some people have more economic value than others – not just for themselves, but for communities and regions and nations. The engine driving the economy is people, but it's not *all* people. It's the Talent.

Richard Florida described cities as being "spiky" – places with talent attract more talent and have faster and stronger economic growth, while everyone else loses what talent they had and fall farther and farther behind. To those who have much, much will be given. To the rest of you... good luck.

—

I used to believe that. And when I wrote the first version of this book, I thought about this as a fact of the matter.

I was wrong.

—

When the Industrial Era was just getting underway, the first generations to go to work in the factories didn't know how to be industrial workers. Pre-industrial farmers ordered their work by the sun and the seasons. Church bells might tell you when to do your religious obligations, but other than that, you went largely by natural signs and what felt right for the time of the day. Pre-industrial farmers and craftspersons generally worked on their home property, with children underfoot. Those children were learning the skills they would use in their adulthood by watching their family members and gradually taking on more and more challenging parts of the process.

Those first generations of industrial workers not only had to learn to tell time (the giant clocks on many old factories testify to that new task), but they had to learn to clock in and out at specific minutes. To take pre-scheduled breaks and meals. To travel to work at a distance from their homes. To live in cities independent of their families. To learn complex tasks in a short time period from a stranger -- a trainer or a work supervisor -- or even more radically, later, from a written manual.

Getting this body of new employees equipped to do all of these new things took more than installing clocks and whistles. It required new housing types. New work roles, like supervisor or trainer. New transportation systems. Not to mention, a complete overhaul of national systems of education so that all those new employees could read the clocks and the manuals.

Early on, before the public parts of those systems all got into place, individual businesses had to help their employees learn these new skills. Otherwise they would have had very, very few employees capable of doing the job. Even though 19th century companies had notoriously little regard for the health of their employees, and certainly did only the bare minimum necessary to get the results they wanted, businesses built housing, held classes, ran trolleys and more for a simple reason: unless they made those investments, they could not get the employees that they needed.

--

Many businesses and organizations have made strides since 2013 in opening their employment to people who were treated as non-Talent in the past. In tight labor markets and high-demand industries, companies will increasingly pay the right person for training, teach the higher-level soft skills necessary for working together in diverse teams, solicit and publish confidential feedback on the degree to which the organization supports diversity, etc. And on the public sector side, "workforce" development has become a specialization within economic development-related work, focusing on job preparedness ranging from adults to middle school.

But despite this, job tenure drops and job satisfaction stagnates across a wide variety of measures, even during recessions. Why?

—

Post - 2013, I led a team that developed a plan for a Power Plant (a community-driven, diversity-powered innovation center) in a midwestern city. One of the community leaders' primary motivations in supporting this work was to increase their Talent supply. They had tried recruiting, which hadn't generated much, and now the call was to help the city's residents, especially its growing number of young, non-white residents, to become long-term employees of the community's businesses.

In preparing the strategy, I interviewed an HR manager at the city's biggest and oldest employer, a company that's a household name. We talked for about 10 minutes about how important innovation was for this company, how central "innovation" was to their business plan. Encouraged, I started to explore ways that the proposed Power Plant could support their goals -- the training, the unique experiences, all of the ways that we could accelerate innovation inside and outside this company.

To which she responded, "Oh! We can't have them take work time to do training and innovation. Who would run the lines?"

And I crash-landed back in the Industrial Era.

Expecting this crucial new Talent to come to us perfectly formed, fully equipped, dropped into a role with a minimum of training is like asking my son when he was five to do algebra. He hadn't learned that yet. But it's also like asking my son at 18 to amuse himself with a wooden train. It's not just a matter of skills, it's a matter of mindset.

If we have been talking about, yelling about, crowing about "Innovation" for the last however many years, and then we put people who have been raised with that message in sit-down-and-do-what-you're-told environments, it's no wonder that so many are disaffected, pessimistic, unwilling to commit to the effort to buy into your offerings, whether it's a job or a public meeting. They believe, reasonably so, that all your big talk has nothing behind it. And in their guts, the most talented know that it's not worth their energy.

It's time to build Fusion Era businesses and organizations that can capitalize on Fusion Era Talent.

Food for Thought

Who is the under-used Talent in your community?

What are they really good at doing?

If you don't know, I recommend you start asking people who might.

Does the Talent want what we're offering?

This section is edited from a piece written by my good friend Bill Lutz, who was a community development manager in a pretty forward-thinking small city in the early 2010s. Bill captures the essence of that conflict between available Talent and existing assumptions and systems -- and sets it in the framework of ongoing generational change.

Too often the actions of community leaders in the field, on the ground, reflect old and unspoken assumptions about what a community needs for its economy. And as Bill points out, in a different way than anything else I have read on this topic, our assumptions about something as fundamental as what it is that the Talent wants may be diverging from reality.

—

Last month, a nearby city collected a major win in the game of economic development. A nutritional supplement maker decided to build a new production plant for one of their products in this small community. The project will lead to the building of a new $270 million facility and create in excess of 200 jobs. These are substantial and impressive figures.

Each week, drive by the site and each week there is more and more progress on this massively large building. But I can't help but wonder if this facility is creating the jobs that our future employees will want to fill.

Is *any* project that promises hundreds of jobs creating the jobs that future employees will want to fill?

I know it's almost sacrilegious to ask such questions in the heartland of American manufacturing, and there's no shortage of people out there who would be glad to take any job, not matter what. But in terms of the people that we keep identifying as the Talent, I think these are more open questions than we want to admit.

Ask anyone currently managing manufacturing industries, and you'll hear the same refrain: there are not enough qualified people to fill the jobs that are out there. That sounds counter intuitive, given the relatively high unemployment rates. Looking at those that are younger, the unemployment rates are even higher. And we increasingly attribute that to a Job-Skills Mismatch, and try to redouble efforts to provide new, better, more sophisticated training.

And yet, these gaps persist — and they persist so broadly that it's clearly more than a one-industry problem. There's something more pervasive here, even after we account for the usual complaints of less-than-ideal literacy skills, work ethic, drug testing, etc.

> What I am starting to believe is that the jobs we are creating aren't the types of jobs the next generation wants or needs to fill.

All of those issues might be factors, and more. But I think it's too convenient to simply blame this generation's perceived lack of work ethic or poor education. I am sure my grandfather's generation thought my father's peers were a bunch of slack-jawed hippies who couldn't carry their own weight.

What I am starting to believe is that the jobs we are creating aren't the types of jobs the next generation wants or needs to fill.

If you read a broad cross-section of the regional and national press about economic development issues, two themes emerge pretty consistently:

#1: Economic developers all across the country are tripping over themselves to get big businesses to come to town -- and often throwing a lot of money at them in the hopes that this will make something happen.

#2: Young job seekers, particularly the ones that we identify as our potential Talent, aren't interested in working for big corporate conglomerates. There's growing evidence - and there has been for a decade or more - that post-Boomer workers are looking for something very different from the Organization Man model that most corporations still hew to in their practices... even if the promises that were supposed to come with Organization Man employment can no longer be trusted.

Take those two statements together, and you get a very different sense of where the problem might lie.

The post-Boomer generations of workers grew up in turbulent times. In many parts of the U.S. and the world, they saw their parents and other adults lose their jobs, whether it was the manufacturing collapse of the 1970s and 80s or the corporate restructuring of the 1980s and 1990s. Job loss wasn't invented in 2008 - the post-Boomer generations, to a large extent, never had reason to develop faith in the corporation.

> They know that their parents had been told that theirs were supposed to be career jobs, but it didn't turn out that way.

In part due to the lack of these jobs, many in this generation grew up with their mothers going to work leading to another generational phenomenon: the latchkey kid. These were the kids that came home from school to an empty house, and it was in these few hours a day that these kids learned to be self-reliant.

So can we honestly be surprised when we see that the most talented of this generation of self-reliant individuals reject the job offers of big business when they come to town, or don't last when they discover what a mismatch there is between their guts and these places?

There's lots of information, both legitimate and sort of pop culture-ish, that claims that post-Boomer workers demand to be flexible and agile. They want to continually build new skills and new abilities, and if necessary, many are willing to do it on their own. Fewer and fewer of these workers seem to be interested in signing up for a job, only to be pigeon-holed in a dead end — especially with the ever-present risk of a pink slip handing over their head.

We keep trying to get more jobs, more economic development. But potentially the biggest problem, and the one that no one seems to be addressing, is that this approach to economic development may fail to answer a much more significant question:

Are the communities we live in attracting the kind of jobs and careers we need if we want to sustain our communities' futures?

Elitism Kills Innovation.

Adapted from Everybody Innovates here, 2018.

Most innovation-focused organizations and businesses don't think of themselves as elitist or exclusionary. Most of them make a point of saying that they are open to everyone, and more and more are actively trying to recruit diverse members (especially the organizations that have a tech focus, since that industry has received so much bad press for hiring predominantly white and male).

But claiming inclusivity and offering an inclusion-supporting experience are not the same thing.

Any organization or business can undercut its claim of inclusivity through a variety of seemingly mundane details. An incubator that lacks closed-off conference rooms with decent soundproofing can make life miserable for a team that comes from a culture where people argue animatedly. A program that relies on retired executives to coach entrepreneurs from disadvantaged communities may find that the experience causes more confusion for its participants than it helps because of unmanaged cultural assumptions. An event series that claims to welcome everyone, but hosts a conference where only one panel member is from a minority population, sets itself up to be

> Any organization or business can undercut its claim of inclusivity through a variety of seemingly mundane details.

viewed with skepticism. And an organization whose board of directors consists of 10 white men and one Asian woman may be projecting a very clear, if perhaps not intentional, message about who is and who is not welcome here.

For many people, these kinds of insensitivities have an ethical component - they should not happen because they are not a good way to behave in the 21st century. But these kinds of inadvertent elitism also create very practical, very damaging leakages:

1. One of the common complaints laid against startups is that many startups spend *hundreds of hours and thousands of dollars to build things that are only useful to a small population* - often one that looks a lot like themselves. For years, I have been a volunteer coach for an entrepreneurship "pitch" event at a large university. Every year, I end up reviewing 20 or 30 business concepts... and every year more than half of them are directly aimed at the narrow market of college students facing some specific challenge that they encountered earlier in the school year.

   I don't blame these student teams for designing a solution to their own needs -- that's a hallmark piece of advice for entrepreneurs. The problem is that *they don't have a wide enough view of the world to empathize with,* and thus perhaps identify innovations for, people who don't look or sound like they do.

Early on in this book I noted that one of our learnings from Econogy was that *diverse teams find better solutions.* An innovator who only knows people who look and sound like her will limit her pursuit of a worthwhile challenge to solve - she will limit it to the problems that face people who look and sound like her. If she had a wider understanding of the world, and if she had the opportunity to co-create with people who come from a different background, she might find her eyes open to a much more valuable (and profitable) opportunity.

So when we inadvertently limit our Innovation Infrastructure to a narrow range of innovators, we effectively deprive them of some of the tools that they need to do innovations that are worth doing.

2. People who have been systematically or routinely excluded, overlooked or disrespected are unlikely to tell you to your face-- especially if they feel that they need your help or acceptance or they don't know whether you will take criticism well. So in many cases, the leaders of the organization that has inadvertently excluded people may never know what impact they have had.

But the people who have been on the receiving end of that experience seldom forget - and the trust needed for collaboration is broken, again denying the larger innovation community of the benefits of rich diversity. Restoring trust in the diverse innovation community, just like in any relationship, requires a long-term dedication to transparency, honesty, and determined effort to improve.

> Restoring trust in the diverse innovation community, just like in any relationship, requires a long-term dedication to transparency, honesty, and determined effort to improve.

> **Food for Thought**
>
> How might your organization be pushing away potential diverse innovators?
>
> How are your practices and assumptions potentially blocking you from benefiting from new ideas?

Who is a potential Innovator?

Adapted from Everybody Innovates here, 2018.

Given that we are focusing on Future Ready innovation, it might make sense to talk about What or Where this kind of innovation can occur or be encouraged. And since we are talking about a new approach, some might think we should start with Why.

But I'm going to start with Who, not just because that's the way we learned the list in elementary school. Putting Who at the center of this description is necessary for several reasons:

- In the emerging economy, **Who is more at the center than ever before**. Innovation is a function of human creativity -- not capital, not real estate, not street trees, not granting programs. Whether we succeed or fail in this era will depend more than ever in human history on whether people can invent solutions, solve problems, and invent the things that we don't know yet that we need.

- **Who often gets overlooked** because we still have this Industrial-era wiring that tells us that the Organization drives progress. We invoke the Who, assert that we are serving the Who, write our grant applications around how we will impact the Who. And sometimes programs and organizations do manage to focus on Who, but too often they focus on individual Whos in an individual moment, without looking to the larger emerging trends and how to build a powerful engine of Whos to capitalize on those emerging trends.

- Just as Startup and Design Thinking and a host of other new business strategies taught us, **Who is the element of our organization or program where we will learn, and thus create better products,** the most. Who, and especially Who as a diverse and inclusive whole, may see what we cannot.

Of course, sometimes Who can be stuck in the present or the past, trying to cling to something familiar or unreflectively applying an out of date rule they internalized years ago, and they may need some help from the program or organization to break out of those mindsets. But the people involved, inherently, provide our best chance, collectively, to create something new and worthwhile.

So... Who?

Adapted from Everybody Innovates here, 2018.

Who has a very short answer: everybody. At least, everybody who can innovate. That means:

- Young people
- Old people
- People of color
- White people
- People who are poor
- People who are wealthy
- People who are female
- People who are male
- People who are not neurotypical
- People who are neurotypical
- People who have high level technical skills
- People who have "street" skills
- People who didn't finish high school
- People who have PhDs
- People who work for themselves
- People who work for Fortune 100 companies
- People who want to work on something Big
- People who want to work on something Small
- People who are fully inside the community
- People who participate occasionally
- People who know what they are trying to achieve
- People who are still looking for the thing they should achieve.
- People who are passionate about something.
- People who want to grow, learn, succeed.
- People who want to do something that matters

If you can think of some more, add them.

Why aren't we getting powerful innovation out of all the money we are putting into it?

Adapted from Everybody Innovates here, 2018.

As we discussed before, almost no existing organization or business is really tapping the full extent of the Talent that could be available to it.

Some businesses or incubators or programs may involve people whose skin comes in a wide variety of colors, but they are all "tech" people or "scale" people or "microenterprise" people. Some may say that they welcome everyone, but their traditional after-class trip to a loud bar excludes the person on the autism spectrum or the working mother who can't afford a $10 drink.

Some claim to include everyone, but they effectively bar the doors to the intrapreneur who needs reinforcement in order to have the impact that he has the unique ability to create - because that person isn't a "starter," in the assumed sense of being a self-dependent entrepreneur.

In most cases, our organizations and businesses are falling short on Who because of one of a few reasons.

- Our "mission" has been to serve one or another subset of innovators. In other words, our Industrial-Era wiring tells us that we have to **stick to our narrow lane,** even if that promises declining returns in a Fusion Era.

- Our "mission" has been to serve those who are disadvantaged and thus we assume that they can't play on the same field as others. In other words, our Industrial-Era wiring tells us that the historically disadvantaged need "help" and don't have **valuable insights that the rest of us need** in our routine innovative lives.

- We have never spent time with a certain population segment, and thus **we didn't know how they could improve everyone else's insight**.

Psychologists have identified three core types of diversity:

- Origin (your skin color, hair color, height, etc.)
- Experience (your life history, what you have experienced)
- Cognitive (how you tend to think and perceive the world)

If finding the solutions that we need requires new ways of thinking and solving, and if diverse groups are more likely to find creative solutions than unilateral groups, then it makes sense that a Future-Ready Innovation District will include the absolute most diverse range of people it can get.

Having said this, though, don't read it as an endorsement of the "Collision" theory of innovation. We talked about this previously, but to recap: Just because you put diverse people in the same physical place does not mean that they will interact.

Our deep-rooted tendencies to tribalism mean that we are far less likely of our own volition to seek out an interaction with someone who looks, sounds or acts different from ourselves, and we're more likely to regard them from the start with fear or suspicion. "Collisions" might happen occasionally, but they are far more likely to happen among two very similar people than among people who are significantly different. The idea that setting a stage conducive to "collision" will make innovation happen is Magical Thinking, especially if the type of innovation we are seeking is bigger than just another widget of marginal value.

Just because you put diverse people in the same physical place does not mean that they will interact.

So the great challenge that a fully diverse Who creates is one of enabling that Who to fully unlock their potential.

Machinery of Innovation

For my co-founder and I, the purpose of Econogy was to accelerate innovation for the places and people we care most about. That includes universities and neighborhoods, businesses and nonprofits, wealthy and disadvantaged, students and seniors. We focused our first two years on building a new machinery of innovation: a system for unlocking the capabilities and lack of barriers that one of the overlooked source of innovation - young adults - could bring to problem-solving.

We found that a **support structure that combined diverse teams, clear processes, and high-stakes stretch challenges resulted in practical but innovative solutions** to problems that had no cookie-cutter answers. From both a business and a human development standpoint, the results were better than we (well, I, at least) anticipated.

We then tried the same methods with adults of varying ages faced with creating strategies for their community's future, and we had similar results.

Consistently, people outperform our expectations when we place around them a structure that enables them to solve problems collaboratively and constructively. And innovation research has found the same:

- **Diverse teams consistently make better decisions**,[5] potentially because they "alter the behavior of a group's social majority in ways that lead to improved and more accurate group thinking."[6]

- When **teams use explicit structured processes to evaluate choices and make decisions, they are more likely to succeed.** Conversely, when leaders assume that the team will just figure it out for themselves - what I've called elsewhere "playing by the rules we learned in kindergarten" - then the team is more likely to fail.[7]

- Creating useful solutions to problems that do not have direct precedents require a fundamentally different approach than simply tweaking things that have been done before. And **being too familiar with the things that have been done before can be like a pair of blinders**, making it impossible to see feasible alternatives that fall outside your expectations.[8]

At Econogy, these experiences gave us proof of concept on something bigger: we had a small but accumulating body of evidence about how we could enable people to

---

5

https://www.hcamag.com/hr-news/do-diverse-teams-perform-better-245514.aspx
[6] https://hbr.org/2016/11/why-diverse-teams-are-smarter
[7] https://hbr.org/2010/06/the-decision-driven-organization
[8]https://www.forbes.com/sites/stevedenning/2012/11/12/why-the-paradigm-shift-in-management-is-so-difficult/#4dc88c935f9

accelerate innovation.

For someone who had spent over 20 years trying to improve problem-solving in communities as a downtown revitalization, urban planning and economic development specialist, this was the kind of insight I'd been looking for. You see, I'd become trapped by my own, conventional understanding of how economies and teams work, too.

Before co-founding Econogy, I had written a lot of lines in a lot of blogs and articles and books about how local economies needed to change, and how the ways we were pushing that to happen weren't working. I had spent hundreds of hours with tech startups, mom and pop shops, universities, microentrepreneurs, and the organizations that try to take care of them. And I knew we needed something different.

But I didn't know what.

After two years of working out the mechanisms for supporting diverse team innovation, and combining that with decades of experience with economic and community support organizations, I've come to the conclusion that **most cities need empowered innovation districts to accelerate innovation across the complete economic and community spectrum.**

There's a lot of different kinds of organizations in this process, and they go by different names in different places. So for sake of simplicity, we're going to call all of these organizations part of the Innovation Infrastructure.

An Innovation Infrastructure, as we are describing it, is a program, a place or a group of programs and places that play a role in generating more economic activity from the people who are in a community. These might include anything from a tech accelerator to a rural organic agriculture collaborative, from a university advanced manufacturing initiative to corporate new initiatives group to a peer coaching program for African-American urban residents who want to start businesses.

That's a radical statement, in case you didn't notice. Historically, we have carefully parsed these segments apart -- tech programs over here, Main Street business owners over here, rural here, urban there, bigger businesses often off by themselves. We differentiate them based on how much money they might make, where their clients live, where they will have their shop, whether we designate them as having a "social impact," and more. And yes, they will have certain needs that are specific to their unique situation.

But what we find over and over is this: **Innovators are often more similar than different.** They all need help innovating. They all need help getting out of their own paradigm. And **they can all learn from each other.**

Talent Systems, Stat.

Human diversity and inclusion are two of the most powerful tools we have to solve the tough problems that have been eluding us -- for the simple reason that no one person can have all the information and experiences and insights within her or himself alone to crack through the barriers that have been blocking us. Whether social, political, environmental... we are in desperate need of paradigm changes, and we know from history that paradigm changes don't come from insiders.

But our skill sets for capitalizing on diversity and inclusion are among our worst, overall. We do a terrible job of using those benefits. Our deep-seated assumptions about who has relevant knowledge and who doesn't, whose voice should be heard and whose should be held in a box labelled "input or "research," who should make the decisions and who should accept them and go along with them....

Our assumptions are outdated. They have been wrecked by poor use. They lack legitimacy in a world that senses, that knows, that there is a big something missing.

But we don't have the skills and the language and the systems to pull that something missing out into the open.

So the block continues to grow, and the problems continue to fester, across nearly every aspect of the modern world.

- Corporations seeking big breakthroughs find very few of them, despite millions of dollars and hours spent chasing them.

- Small businesses and entrepreneurs flounder in mental isolation, spending precious years on solutions that don't accurately fit the kind of problems that matter.

- Nonprofits and other organizations that are trying to solve tough problems cannot get past twiddling at the edges, or they limit their impact to one small corner of the world and fail to spread to the extent of the actual need.

- And governments, everyone's favorite whipping post, struggle to provide what they need to provide in a poisoned environment, in part of their own making.

In a world that has so many unmet, acute, urgent needs - needs that solving would unlock real value -- why aren't we doing it?

Some pundits may pin it on human self-centeredness, or Machiavellian political urges, or the fact that new ideas are just *hard.* But we've done hard and noble and groundbreaking things before. We're doing them now -- just not enough and not fast enough.

The root source of our current blocks isn't technical - we have technologies that our grandparents could not have imagined. It's not strictly political - governments have driven great strides in human health and well being in the past 200 years. And it's not that people have somehow fundamentally shifted from effective to floundering: despite the hand wringing in the daily news, we know that there's nothing new under the sun in human behavior and morals. Across the millennia to today, what we're seeing is mostly variations on a theme.

The core difference now is that the **issues that bedevil us lie beyond the scope of what we could address with our Industrial Era tools** -- specialization, hierarchy, efficiency, professionalism. The biggest issues facing us cross a range of scientific or technical bailiwicks, demonstrating the most need at the intersections of the topics that we have carefully divided from each other by degrees and professional memberships.

And increasingly, the division between the human mind and heart -- the emphasis on rational solutions over intuition, intellectual solutions over the human need for solidarity and stability, analytical and design-informed methods of problem-solving -- all of these create magma domes under our collective rational exteriors. Those divisions threaten, they sow fear, they further block real solutions, they twist decision-making and solution-doing in ways that can undercut more than they solve.

The core challenge in front of us in the new economic/social/cultural era that is dawning is to take apart our no-longer-necessary blocks and learn to harness human creativity, human learning, and the full range of human insight in ways that we have not before. This means that our basic methods for how we do the work of advancing humanity is going to have to become very different, just as the skills we used to harvest rye in the 1600s bore little resemblance to the Ford assembly line of the 1910s. That's the kind of profound everything-change we're going to have to undergo.

But we don't have a few hundred years to fight through the transition this time. Between global warming and global urbanization and a host of other significant challenges, our window for a successful transition is a whole, whole lot shorter.

—

I don't know how to solve all those global challenges, but I have learned that the **best way to find genuinely new solutions is most clearly seen at the opposite end of the scale from the global: in groups of people who bring the most diverse possible range of skills, experiences, outlooks and perspectives to work together in in true collaboration** - I often say co-creation. These are the kinds of teams that find, understand and figure out how to use the treasures in the spaces in between our individual domains.

But we don't do that by the seat of the pants. We aren't genetically wired or culturally acclimated to work with people who are different from us. Both our in-bred defensive mechanisms and our cultural learning actually pushes, hard, against that kind of openness. We came up as tribal people, after all, and Us vs. Them lies deep in our psyches.

But us vs them looks pretty likely to take us all out, if we don't learn to work around it.

We've done this before - agriculture, formal education, social niceties, riding a bicycle, all required us to work around our urges and assumptions and long-learned behaviors from earlier eras. And often those long-learned behaviors had to do with fear of others. We can certainly do it again.

But **co-creation with diverse people is a learned skill, not an innate talent**. If we truly intend to capitalize on our potential, to find the solutions to the tough problems, we can't keep doing it the same way. We need to build, learn, teach and use new ways of working together. And we have to replace our old methods with the systems, the processes, the paradigms that reinforce this new approach. And that's not just an exercise for the classroom, or the corporate office, or for the city council chambers. It's in all of them, across all of them.

We can do this. But we have to start. As soon as we can.

Bonus Undercurrent for People Who Do Economic Development or Urban Planning

Throughout this book, I've made some critique of economic developers and planners, and their professions. Which can feel sketchy for me because I am both myself, or at least a hybrid, and I'm writing this as a help for people who care about a community, whether that's their job or not. But in this section I need to talk some inside ball, and point out how these Undercurrents are setting these professions up to fail, if we don't change our professional paradigms as well.

The fiscal crunches and budget cuts of the last few years have made "economic development" part of pretty much everyone's job, if they have a place that they care about. From the city manager to the council member, the nonprofit board, the guy who runs the co working space, even the coffee shop owner who sells "We Love Our Town" stickers, we're all somehow "doing" economic development. Sometimes doing it with more impact than the professional economic developers.

Similarly, more and more people seem to be paying attention to traditionally urban planning issues, like the density of new developments and the impacts on traffic and the need or folly of extended mass transit. A new player, called an "urbanist," begins to weigh in, perhaps proposing a strategy called Tactical Urbanism that uses cheap temporary materials to create potential improvements, largely circumventing conventional studies and projections in favor of simply trying it on.

These trends should be welcomed, because we all want engaged and motivated residents. But from a professional and a self-preservation point of view, that should make the card-carrying economic developers and planners pretty damn nervous.

So the next few pages are geared specifically to economic development and urban planning professionals. Everyone else can go get a sandwich or something.

But in case you worry that you'll be missing something, here's the Cliff Notes version: Most of the other professions and roles and people-types that deal with communities are starting to work on economic development or urban planning issues. And that's often because they don't see any benefit to what economic developers or planners claim to do. And in a lot of cases, they're angling for the same pots of money, the same political and corporate support, the same basic community role, as you usually tap.

And in many cases, they're doing a freaking good job of it.

Don't shoot the messenger.

—

OK, guys, just you and me for a moment.

Are they gone yet? Good.

One of the most uncomfortable things that I have had to say to economic development and planning professionals lately is that I'm not all that much worried about communities as a whole (certain ones worry me a lot). There are thousands of people in the U.S. who do things related to improving local economies – from organizers working with neighborhoods, to people running accelerators, to the growing number of self-organized groups that can kick change in a community into gear simply by their numbers and the ease with which internet technologies allow them to communicate and work in concert.

The big question to me at the moment is, where are economic development and planning professionals going to fit into that evolution, and what impact will it have on people and on communities if the profession, and those professionals, simply become irrelevant?

Economic Development and Life on the Playground

Economic development seems to be more about the process than the product. From my perspective as a low-key half-time ED professional, economic development is nearly 85-90% about marketing and relationship building. I understand how these activities can play a role, but it's a role that seems too pronounced. What exactly are we marketing and how are these relationships going to help?....

We get all excited when the new report comes out, or the new branding initiative hits or the new restaurant breaks ground...when do we go back and measure the effectiveness of those efforts? Are those jobs created by the restaurant moving the needle? Does that watering hole become a community asset?

-An email correspondent after a blog post. Used by permission but name withheld by request.

More process than product, and more output than outcome. The point is pretty damning: from the writer's perspective in the trenches, the economic development profession doesn't seem to be actually making a difference.

'Scuse me while I squirm for a minute.

———

It's hard not to see some truth in what this writer is saying.

The profession of economic development started out, historically, as a sales job. Our mission was to entice businesses to come to your town or your state. Close the deal. Get the win. And you don't have to spend a lot of time around economic developers to know that for many professionals, and many communities, selling is still the primary definition of the job. Going and schmoozing and relationship-building... it's fundamentally the same work that the business development director of a company does. Make the sell, or make the connection that down the road might lead to a sell.

But the sell – the win – too easily becomes the name of the game. Sure, the targets are usually smaller than they were in the halcyon days, and now we allocate at least some of our effort to trying to make that sell to our local businesses so that they don't pick up and go somewhere else. But fundamentally, for many economic development professionals and organizations, the sell is still the purpose of the job.

> It can be pretty easy to sell someone something that they don't need, and it's awfully easy to sell someone something that you cannot or should not try to supply.

There's a problem with sales, and I say this as someone who tries to sell professional services every day: it can be pretty easy to sell someone something that they don't need, and it's awfully easy to sell someone something that you cannot or should not try to supply.

For economic development, it's that second element that's making me more and more uneasy. The purpose of economic development, fundamentally, isn't just selling more and more and more. The purpose of economic development is to support the places that we live and work and play in – to improve their economies, help their people make a living, build the tax base that they need so that places can be kept clean and safe and comfortable.

That's why governments and communities and businesses fund these things.

I think we've all had to admit in the last 20 years, at least to ourselves, that some of our economic development "wins" didn't turn out to be wins at all – or at least not the happy, unambiguous wins that we might have told ourselves they were. Gave a sweet deal to a big box store and now you discover that your other commercial spaces are going dark? Recruited a distribution center and now you're finding that the rate of police and ambulance calls there are far higher than expected?

Provided tax increment financing for a shiny new office building, and now your city council is cutting your operating budget because tax revenue isn't keeping up with service demands?

In a lot of cases, it's pretty clear in hindsight that we sold something that we shouldn't have sold – at least, not for the cheap price or with the bells and whistles that we sold it. And sometimes it seems like we're not learning from our mistakes.

There are a lot of people who are doing good, thoughtful work in economic development – who are connecting the importance of their work to the health of their communities. There are people and communities who are trying to anticipate and head off the potential unintended consequences that some economic development projects present, and there are people and communities who are shifting toward a holistic perspective, toward growing a local economy that can provide its residents with long-term stability and resilience.

But then... there is the view from my correspondent's window, and that of others who write to me out of frustration. And it's not the view I want them to see, or the view that I want to be shown. It frames an uncomfortable lack of critical thinking, a failing to learn from the past mistakes of the profession, and a tendency to overlook or ignore the ways in which new projects and exciting proposals can create more problems for the community we're working for than they solve.

Instead, the view from their window shows a playground-style tally sheet: points for me on this side, points for you on that side. Get more points in my column than yours, and I win! Simple as that.

Except that winning at that game may actually do no good at all

Scratch a Planner...

If you have heard me speak any time in the last 20 years, I would guess you have heard me say this:

Scratch a planner, find a dictator underneath.

That was a favorite quote from my graduate school economics professor, who had found himself stranded in a school of planning (academic careers can be strange). It came from a footnote in an economics text (for the life of me, I haven't been able to find that text). And after 20 years in the School of Planning, he would repeat that quote on occasion with a slight twisted smile. But no additional content.

It became a sort of koan. It didn't make much sense, but it obviously meant something.

When I finally went to work as a planner, I was over 30 and starting a new career. I had worked briefly in journalism and in middle school classrooms, and spent about 6 years doing historic preservation and heritage tourism work. I had a new master's degree in Planning, but most of my professional formation had occurred in other contexts. I've had a theory for a long time that what you do in your 20s sets in place a lot of how you will approach your work, regardless of whether you stay in the same career or not. And although I had changed careers all over the place, by the time I became a planner, I suspect that much of my mindset was already formed. And formed differently from most of my colleagues, who came straight out of their undergrads into planning jobs.

I landed at a consulting firm that developed comprehensive plans and zoning codes and the like for U.S. Midwestern cities. But like most degree programs, planning school teaches you foundations and theories, and is often light on real world applications. So I found myself managing the development of comprehensive plans, but without having spent my 20s working on them and absorbing the standard operating procedures.

One day early in my planning life, I came out of my office to our common work area to find one of my colleagues working on a draft map for one of our plans (at this point we still did a lot of the initial map work on paper and then handed it to the GIS specialists to create digital versions). Andy had a neatly lined up row of markers to his right, a large plot of the base map in front of him, and he was making circles and arrows and coloring in shapes and making notations in that beautiful architectural-style lettering that everyone I had met who had an undergraduate in planning knew how to do (my lettering scrawled and never stayed on a straight line, just as it had on a chalkboard or my reporter's notebook).

As he worked, Andy was beaming. I'd never seen him so happy. Not at the dozens of community meetings we had done, not even when joking around in the kitchen. Drawing those circles and arrows was the personal high point of the plan creation experience for him.

I didn't get it.

But I got an inkling as to what my professor's koan meant.

———

There's something satisfying about creating a plan. You have a vision of the future laid out before you, pristine and perfect, uncomplicated, logical, ideal. I think Andy's happiness, and that of a lot of other planners I have known, came from the act of creating something that was, in its own way, beautiful.

But of course, plans don't stay pristine and perfect once you try to bring the ideal into messy reality. The Victor Gruen story I told in a previous chapter gave a prime lesson in that.

I wonder sometimes whether the planner's love of the plan, the idealized plan, the concept unsullied by real life, leads to two of the critiques most commonly leveled at plans:

Lack of meaningful public input, and

The proverbial plan gathering dust on the shelf.

I've talked about engaging the full range of the public in building the communities we want to have throughout this book to this point, and I'll get into more on that going forward. But I think it's important to call out to my planner colleagues that

> (1) the processes that we call "public engagement" are mostly fundamentally flawed, poorly designed and set up to create conflict, sometimes despite our best intentions,

> (2) these public engagement failures have piled up on themselves for decades, creating ossified layers of distrust in the system and in us, and

> (3) the Undercurrents that we have talked about in Part 1 of this book are pushing harder than ever against our usual ways of dealing with the world outside the Plan.

We usually blame the fact that the plan "gathered dust on the shelf" on Someone Else -- the big deal developer, the power-hungry mayor or city manager, the NIMBYs and BANANAs, and more.

But perhaps a big part of that blame lies with us, with our desire to protect the pristineness of our creations from those messy realities. Perhaps that's why it seems so much easier, and happier, to create our plans at arm's length from the people we are supposedly planning for.

Because we can only be a dictator in our plans when the Plan remains isolated from reality.

Part 2:

Crap. So Now What?

Shall we take a 15 minute break to get a libation of your choice?

That last section could be kind of depressing stuff. The basic assumptions underlying much of what we are doing are wrong? Don't fit anymore? We can't just wait for happy days to come again?

This is a lot harder than I thought.

Yes, it is. But it's not undoable. It's going to take a while, though. So we might as well get started now.

This section will play out four basic implications of the sea changes we talked about in Part 1. We'll start broad again with each one and go more narrow — starting with an element of the paradigm shift that the facts necessitate, and working through to some general principles of practice.

If someone tells you they have an easy answer, rest assured that what they're offering is a magic pill. And you won't find any list of potential side effects on that bottle. Take it at your peril.

Part 2, Implication 1:

Hang up the wrench and pick up the hoe[9]

---

[9] This section might look like it's going to talk about Economic Gardening, but it's not. Economic Gardening is a specific method used to help certain businesses in a community achieve higher potential. That fits with what this section is intended to discuss, but the section uses the gardening metaphor more broadly. To learn more about Economic Gardening methods, check out the National Center for Economic Gardening, economicgardening.org.

The paper machine and the gardener

Photo by Geograph, subject to creative commons license

This is a paper machine. My husband ran one in the 1990s. I've often said it's the only job he ever had where I actually could say what the heck he did all day. He made paper.

A paper machine is a huge hunk of equipment. The whole machine usually extends about a thousand feet from one end to the other, so it's about the length of an urban city block. It has lots of parts that whizz and hiss and rumble and make noises so loud you need ear protection, and sometimes the paper coming off the end of it breaks and sends clouds of fuzzy confetti flying everywhere. It looks like controlled chaos, managed power, in action. It's really kind of cool.

Despite looking so impressive, paper machines do something that's basically pretty simple: they take a slurry of water and paper pulp, and they suck out the water and squash the pulp together to turn it into paper. There are several steps to the process, and sometimes there's lotion or scent or something that gets introduced into it along the way, but fundamentally, that's what the paper machine does. Evaporate and squash.

As you might imagine, a machine this size has tons of controls — levers and inputs and electronic dials, and the technicians who run the thing have to be pretty well trained to keep it all working. But fundamentally, all the pieces that they can manipulate do one of two things: they take water out, or they squash paper fibers together.

We tend too often to think of our local economies as paper machines. We have a handful of levers and dials that we know that we can push or pull, and we assume (or tell ourselves) that we can get the outcomes we want for our local economies by twiddling those controls. Sometimes we call those controls incentives, or new parks, sometimes they're sewer lines or land that we can sell at a deep discount, sometimes they're slick marketing materials designed to show potential businesses that "Hey!!! We are awesome!!!"

The problem is, our communities aren't much like paper machines at all. They're more like forests or farms or gardens.

For a plant to grow requires a wide range of conditions — the right soils, the right amount of rain, the right amount of sun or shade, the right pollinating insects and the absence of the right kind of pests. Some plants have higher ranges of tolerances than others — some of the flowers in my yard, for example, wilt when the temperature gets above 90, while the weeds could apparently survive a nuclear blast.

The main thing that makes a garden different from a paper machine, though, is the degree to which we lack direct control over many of those factors. I can't change the number of hours in a day that the sun shines, and I can't ensure enough of a supply of the pollinators that my fruit trees want if something on the next farm over keeps eating them.

> Not only do we lack direct control, we have to accept the fact that we lack direct control. Berating the sun to stay in the sky longer, or trying to pollinate each apple blossom by hand, don't sound like helpful solutions.

Not only do we lack direct control, we have to accept the fact that we lack direct control. Berating the sun to stay in the sky longer, or trying to pollinate each apple blossom by hand, don't sound like helpful solutions.

—

If we shift away from thinking of communities as machines to manipulate, and we shift toward thinking of them as gardens to manage, that creates a number of implications, some of which we'll explore in the next sections. But here's a few to get started:

- If we are tending the garden, rather than trying to manhandle the machinery, then our role can fit what Brad Feld described in his book about StartUp Communities: **we can readily be feeders, rather than trying to force leadership.** You can't lead a plant to grow — the most effective thing you can do is create the conditions in which it can grow best. If our role is as local economy feeders, then we can concentrate on the things that our existing businesses consistently tell us have the biggest impact on their operations.

- If we are managing the forest, rather than manipulating the machinery, then our role is not to "make deals happen." Our role, instead, is to **enable an environment where good economic stuff can happen.** That means that our resources can reach farther, we can allocate some of our resources to carefully-monitored novel approaches, and we can spread our impact across the community, instead of just hoping that one or two Big Deals will somehow have far-reaching positive impacts.

- If the work of economic development is tending the garden, rather than trying to push something through the machinery, then the proliferating number of smaller deals that currently demand more and more and more of our increasingly squeezed time... **aren't demanding so much of our time.** We know in our guts that we don't have the time or the human-power to give all those smaller businesses the same level of attention. If we shift our focus to strengthening the garden as a whole, rather than trying to meet the demands of each individual business individually, then we can reach more broadly and overcome our staffing and budget limits.

- If the work of economic development is managing the forest, rather than whacking at the buttons on the machine in the hoped-for but unproven belief that somehow pushing the right combination will make everything better, then we **no longer face the pressure to grab anything that comes along, at any cost.** Everyone knows that you can't grow a cypress tree in Fairbanks, Alaska, or keep a birch tree alive very long in the Amazon. If we're doing gardening, rather than trying to directly manipulate the system, then we lose the pressure to sink our limited resources into cultivating pretty but delicate exotics.

That all might sound a little idealistic, and it is — but to make a point. We have generally poor results to show for the Machine Management Model of economic development — and as average business size gets smaller and smaller, and the number of Big Win opportunities shrinks even faster, we're finding that we can pound on the control panel all we want, the machine isn't making our communities better. And it's wearing us out, on top of it.

Reframing, re-orienting our economic development efforts in this manner doesn't just make abstract metaphor sense. It makes practical, how- you-run- your-department-or- organization sense. How much more impact could you ultimately have if you shifted from pushing "deals" through the machine, to enabling businesses to function better?

Native Species

Q: What is this flower?

From wikimedia.org, subject to Creative Commons license.

A: An apple blossom. It's also the state flower of Michigan.

Q: What's this second flower?

A: A Hibiscus. It's also the state flower of Hawaii.

Have you ever tried to grow these two plants in the Midwest? I have. When I lived in Green Bay, Wisconsin (similar climate to Michigan), I had one scraggly apple tree in my backyard - a senior citizen estimated to be about 50 years old. The thing was - no way around it - ugly. Gnarled branches, sort of bent over to one side, unsymmetrical, half-bare. And we did nothing to take care of it.

Despite its looks and our lack of husbandry, every spring, that tree put out a drift of blossoms over its branches, and every fall it produced apples...they tasted awful, but they were apples, nonetheless.

On a recent return visit, we drove by the old house and peeked in the backyard, and there was that same old ugly tree, laden down with fruit.

I don't have an apple tree when I live today in Cincinnati, but I do have a hibiscus tree. It's actually our second hibiscus-- my husband bought a second after the first one finally limped to its demise. We have to keep it in a pot because it can't survive the winters, and we have to stake it up in the pot because it doesn't have a deep enough root system to keep it upright in even a little bit of wind when we do put it outside in the summer. The hibiscus goes through random periods where it drops leaves all over the place, and when it's inside it attracts swarms of little white bugs and a sort of gooey residue. This hibiscus tree has lovely blossoms, when it blossoms, but the rest of the time it's a plain old pain in the neck. It probably would have died in a week in Wisconsin.

To grow an apple tree in northern Wisconsin takes very little effort. To grow a hibiscus in southern Ohio takes a huge amount of effort.

If the goal of your gardening is to produce flowers or fruit, growing an apple tree is going to be a more efficient, less labor-intensive way to meet that goal, in that climate, than growing a hibiscus. They don't look the same, and the one that isn't From Here is always going to look more exotic and enticing. But they both produce flowers, and one produces the results we want in the

If the goal of your gardening is to produce flowers or fruit, growing an apple tree is going to be a more efficient, less labor-intensive way to meet that goal, in that climate, than growing a hibiscus.

climate where we find ourselves much more easily than the other.

———

Conventional approaches to economic development put a huge amount of emphasis on trying to grow exotics in places where they do not naturally grow. We send economic development professionals on trade missions all over the world, we bleed ourselves to be able to announce that we have the lowest tax rates, and we pour millions of dollars into incentives to recruit businesses – or retain them after they are here.

But unless a business needs what we uniquely have to offer, we will never have confidence that we are building for the long run. We can never be sure that they won't pull up and move to the next cheaper place when this load of tax incentives run out.

There are two truths of economic development that we don't often talk about. The first is that very, very, very few businesses relocate in a year, and fewer now than in years past. All of the chasing after site selectors that economic developers often do, all of the money and effort and travel spent trying to land that big businesses...

More and more, it's a hunt for elusive game. There's a reason why wealthy Edwardian big-game hunters went to Africa for safaris: they had a lot of money. You can spend a lot on the thrill of the chase when you have a lot to spend in the first place.

Chasing big business recruitments, for most of us, equals going after a big payoff with extremely long odds. Much of the money spent on the chase will see little, if any, return. To a great extent, reliance on big business recruitment is a bet on the roulette table: fantastic if you hit it, but hardly what you want as your retirement savings strategy.

The other truth of the matter is that most businesses do not primarily choose a location on the basis of tax incentives. When most businesses do go in search of a new location, their first screen is based on their business's needs – regional location, workforce skills, access to transportation, ability to recruit key talent, etc. They will ask for tax incentives because that's part of the dance, and they will threaten to go somewhere else that has better tax breaks because it's in their best interest to get a little more if they can.

Communities seldom win business that they would not otherwise get through tax breaks. Most business' needs are much more complex than that.

———

Given that betting on the exotic requires so much additional effort for such long odds, communities that focus on cultivating the businesses and economic opportunities that grow naturally in their area have a much better chance of long-term economic health and resilience. Your native businesses are the ones that are adapted to your social, cultural and economic environment from the start, and they are the ones who are in the best position to anticipate and adapt to changes in the world surrounding them. They may be humble, even boring, compared to the unusual and flashy from Somewhere Else, but they are your safest bet for long-term growth.

Helicopter-Parenting

When they were young, my kids set up a lemonade stand on the street in front of my house. I encouraged them to do it for all the usual good reasons- introduction to basic market economics, sense of achievement, etc. We live in a very safe neighborhood, but, you know, I'm Mom. I've had too many years of Stranger Danger training. I typically found myself watching them from the front window.

One time, gross sales for the day totaled $8, and someone who thought they were cute paid them $3 for a 50 cent glass of lemonade. Needless to say, it wasn't a mile-a-minute action. And I had a huge urge to step in, get them making bigger signs, go buy them some sparkly banners, *make them more successful.*

While I stood there, I realize that my conflict is a lot like the challenge that we who are responsible for local economies face:

We want to directly control and influence what happens in our communities, but we know we can't. We can't because, at the end of the day, it's not our lemonade stand, even though we might have provided the raw materials and we might have even shaped the environment in which it operates. At the end of the day, we have to let the economy of our community happen. We can guide, cajole, even land some well-placed pushes, but we cannot make it happen.

Sometimes we do try to make it happen- we create incentives, we offset funding gaps, we permit one type of development and prohibit another for the sake of the public welfare. And a lot of the time, the immediate thing that we want to happen, happens.

If I had charged out to the curb and taken control of the lemonade sales, if I had made the kids bigger and fancier signs, or directed them to a more high-traffic location, I bet they would have sold a lot more than 6 glasses. And I wouldn't have had to worry about their safety.

Improved results when the Expert gets involved.

But when we do that, we risk a consequence — and as we are learning more and more these days, we risk a long-term unintended consequence.

If I take over the kids' lemonade stand, they may sell more lemonade, and probably won't get grabbed by a stranger, but they won't learn the lessons from the experience that was the real point of the activity. And if I keep acting like that, and they never learn independence and how the market works, that could have some very serious impacts on their futures.

What about our communities? Do we risk long-term unintended consequences because of our urge to try to control the places that we personally and professionally care about? Can we shift instead to a model of facilitating growth, enabling opportunities, without trying to artificially force them to happen?

> Do we risk long-term unintended consequences because of our urge to try to control the places that we personally and professionally care about?

Sell Saturns, not clunkers

People tell me all the time that the job of an economic developer is to "sell" their community. I think that definition is misleading, and damaging.

When you examine conventional economic marketing methods and materials, you perceive pretty readily that the skill sets for selling a community are, in essence, the same skill sets as selling television sets or cars: communication, persuasion, positive spin, getting people to like you, persistence, closing the sale.

That is the nature of a sales job. I sold professional services for 20 years. I get that.

But we have three problems with "selling" a community like a product or service today. And I suspect that communities who cling to this paradigm will make themselves increasingly irrelevant — and hobble themselves in the process.

The first problem is that the **nature of sales is changing, and changing swiftly and profoundly.** If you don't believe me, go hang out with some marketing or advertising people for a while. Being in a national center of consumer marketing in Cincinnati, I get to be a fly on the wall for these conversations fairly regularly. But a few issues of the magazine _Fast Company_ or _INC._ will give you a taste.

The marketing and advertising professions have been going through gut-wrenching changes - not just because of the shift in media consumption, but because of upheavals in popular expectations about how companies and brands and products should behave - how they should relate to customers and consumers. Marketing gurus now insist that you have to have a dialogue instead of just talking at your customers. You have to engage them, be authentic!! The basic ideas seem to be mostly in place, but professional advertising and sales people are still trying to figure out how to make it work. Read the media coverage of the ads on the last SuperBowl and you'll see what I mean.

The second problem with the old sales model is that the **nature of the audience you're talking to has changed.** They have more sophisticated expectations than they did 20 years ago. They are more likely to look for detailed data, ask probing questions, look at issues that don't show up in your advertising brochures, like your community's political stability. On top of that, for communities that are recognizing the importance of retaining and expanding their existing businesses, a traditional sales models does not work. Try to sell a used car to the person who used to own it, and you'll see what I mean.

The third issue is that the **nature of our responsibility is changing.** We are finally starting to understand that it's all connected--that our communities are interdependent ecosystems, not a thing with separate parts. Housing and parks and community organizations and fiscal structures are all part of economic development--sometimes we call that by the overused term "Quality of Life." When I taught a professional economic development course a couple of weeks ago and asked the students what they were responsible for in their communities, more than one said "quality of life" – an answer I would have never heard 15 years ago.

Quality of life is shorthand for "the stuff that we used to let the planners and park guys and whoever deal with, but now it's what the businesses are asking us about."

You cannot sell your way to quality of life...and you cannot put a sharp marketing effort on a place that doesn't offer what people are looking for when they can go to citydata.com and see the truth about your education rate, or go on Google maps and see how shabby your parks really are.

———

As I have mentioned, my father was a casualty of the early 1980s recession, and spent most of three years trying to find a new job. My father loved cars, and was devoted to both Chrysler and the local dealership franchise that sold Chrysler products. So when he was offered a job selling used cars for that dealer, it looked like a dream come true.

He sucked at it.

In the days before CarFax and blue book prices online, used car selling was closer to horse trading than what we have today. Selling late 1970s and early 80s K cars meant putting a lot of lipstick on pigs, and a lot of haggling over prices. I was pretty young, and he died many years ago, so I don't know all the details. But my theory is that he knew too much about what was under the hoods of these lemons, and as a reasonably upright guy, he couldn't fully commit to what he had to do to sell clunkers to rubes.

Many years later I bought a Saturn (I married into a GM family - there's a rule against inbreeding). Saturn was the first car brand to set its prices without haggling, so the sales process was more about educating the buyer. Saturn put its salespeople in polos and khakis (groundbreaking in itself in the early 1990s), hired younger people and women, equipped them with detailed information on each model, purposely took a low key approach and basically turned your usual assumptions about buying a car on its head. Set pricing and polo shirts and the like are standard parts of the car buying process now, but if you remember the early days of Saturn, their approach was radically disruptive.

I bought my last Saturn in 2007, in the second to last year before GM shuttered the brand (my son still drives it). By that point, my dad had been dead for five years. And in one of those weird moments that hits you out of nowhere when you have lost someone, I choked up in the middle of filling out the paperwork.

The thought that flattened me out of the blue:

Dad would have been a hell of a good Saturn salesman.

———

The Saturn model of sales is hardly innovative in auto sales anymore. But it was a precursor to the demand of transparency and informed customers and insistence on a relationship model that all of the sales-related professions are wrestling with today.

"Look how great we are!!!" does not cut it, and won't. Your potential "buyers," both inside your community and out, don't want a glossy ad. They want information. They want clear information. They want information that they can trust and use to help make better decisions. They *want* to know whether your community is a good fit for their plans. Chances are, they might be thinking more long-term than some of your elected leaders hounding you for quick wins. So if you want the work you do to have meaning, if you want it to make a real difference in your community, don't give in to selling used cars the old way.

Sell Saturns.

Dog Sleds and Little Bets[10]

Check out this examination from Anna Farmery, of The Engaging Brand, a leading thinker about emerging issues in business and marketing in the UK:

> [I]n the digital economy I wonder if as an entrepreneur or business leader should we change our concept of corporate culture?
>
> When the digital age is moving so quickly and consumers are gaining power, maybe the future trend will be towards a disposable company - it launches, it delivers, it morphs into something else or disappears?
>
> In my lifetime I have seen clothes, TV's, phone's etc. come to a price point that makes them almost disposable if you want them to be....
>
> So why not a company?
>
> When the digital age is combined with slow economic growth.....the hockey stick financial plans [picture a graph that shows slow growth followed by a sharp increase at some point in the future] look redundant. Imagine the hockey stick becoming a 2-3 year project? Imagine such a lean, decentralized company that it can move quickly, fold and then come back as something fresh that embraces the new technology?

---

[10] The Little Bets concept in business is the work of Peter Sims and the Little Bets Lab. Learn more at http://littlebetslabs.com/

Maybe, just maybe, we should be focused not on growing structure but on growing flexibility?[11]

From my own notes:

A hell of a question...implications for economic development?

Implications indeed. Think about not just this idea, but what it implies.

We know that employment for many people looks nothing like it looked for my father and my grandfather – so different that even a session at the International Economic Development Council's Leadership Conference can question whether the concept of a "job" still exists. In the early 2010s, the magazine *Fast Company* described a Generation Flux where the most successful careers zigzag across business types. High school students are advised that they may very well spend their careers in industries that don't exist yet.

And the very concept of a business – the foundation of how we think about our local economies – could become an antiquated idea as well.

The woman who wrote for a newspaper 25 years ago on trash paper and a manual typewriter writes this on a glass screen that she holds in one hand and brushes with a finger. And I do that as though I were born to it.

---

[11]Anna Farmery, "Era of Disposable Company?" http://www.theengagingbrand.com/2013/03/era-of-disposable-company.html

Don't tell me that we know what's coming next. If all that doesn't make you nervous, you might not have nerves.

———

Local governments are arguably the most slow-changing creatures on the landscape-- and that's partly prudent and partly by design. If you live off the monies of people who are typically reluctant to give you more, and you have spent three decades in a zeitgeist that suspects you of being a wasteful sloth, you have a monsoon-scale headwind pushing you take it slow, don't get crazy, don't rock the boat.

Add to that a constant, years-long, unrelenting squeeze on budgets, loss of one co-worker after another who used to help you carry that burden, and a constant nagging cold fear about where the budget cuts will fall next, and it's no wonder at all that our community's professionals can barely get their heads around the day-to-day issues facing them, let alone figure out how to work in the upset-the-apple-cart world I just described.

And most businesses, with their pressures to operate lean and Six Sigma and Kaizen, aren't internally much better equipped to handle an unpredictable but very different future coming down the track.

I've said before that we need to fundamentally change how we do governance, business economic development. But for me, just like for everyone else in the growing chorus singing from that hymnal, this picture hasn't come into focus yet. There's parts that become a little more clear, and huge swaths that lurk in the shadows. Talk about seeing through a glass darkly.

But we can't give up, we have to start figuring it out, unknowns or not. But how? We know the feds aren't going to do this for us, or some well-funded research outfit, or our state's economic development agency.

So what do we do?

———

Here's a small way that we can all start sharpening the picture, for all of us. And I do mean, small.

Businesses that remain successful for the long term continually look forward. And based on what they see -- but knowing that what they think they see could be a mirage or something much different than it appears today -- they make Little Bets.

> Little Bets stick a toe into a place where we don't know what they will find, and by doing that they help us get a little more insight into the situation.

Little Bets sometimes sound like experiments, but I think that's the wrong comparison. They're more like probes... they stick a toe into a place where they don't know what they will find, and by doing that they help us get a little more insight into the situation.

But -and here is probably the critical part, especially for something complicated like the future of our communities - they aren't intended to be permanent.

———

Robert Peary led the first team of explorers to reach the North Pole in 1909. Think about how you do an expedition like that. You don't send a team to the North

Pole for the first time and equip them to all stay there for 20 years. The exploration team goes part of the way,, they check out the environment and the landscape, they learn things, they come back, the next effort builds on that new knowledge.

In Peary's case, the 1909 team actually built from a series of previous expeditions through the Arctic – earlier probes that, while incomplete in themselves, made the North Pole exploration possible.

There's a tactical reason to explore unknown territory that way, and there's also a very pragmatic economic reason:

What would cost less, sending a few guys with sled dogs to the North Pole, or establishing a North Pole Program, setting them up to live in an unknown and dangerous environment for 20 years?

As crazy risky as arctic exploration was 100 years ago, those risks were nothing compared to what they would have encountered if they tried to set up a city with what little they knew about the place. Imagine all the things that could have gone wrong. By comparison, sending a small team to go there and then turn around and coming back would have looked relatively easy. And cheap.

Robert Peary with sled dogs. Cheaper than a Program. From the Frederick Cook collection, Ohio State University Library. http://library.osu.edu/

Peary's expedition to the North Pole was a series of probes. It was a system of Little Bets.

—

A Little Bet differs subtly but substantially from what we usually do, whether within a government or through a non-profit community partner.

We tend to try to build our programs full grown from Day 1: staff, offices, missions, strategic plans, whole ball of wax. And that means two things:

First, **we sink costs into the new thing that makes it Permanent**. And Permanence creates both a barrier to starting ("Another program?") and a barrier to changing ("But we don't do that...").

Second, we **overestimate what we know and our ability to predict the future.** That's human nature. We got away with it when economies were more predictable and life seemed simpler- or at least, when we could let ourselves think that way. But when we think we know what the future looks like, we invest more time, and people, and emotion, and money, into the thing we build. And when something doesn't work quite like we thought, we're stuck.

Try to unpack and reload a warehouse, and then do the same with a dog sled. You'll see what I mean.

———

We would all be better off if every government, every nonprofit, every funder, put a tiny share of its budget - my first guess, less than 5 percent, or maybe no more than you spend on office supplies - and put that each year toward one carefully chosen Little Bet. Treat it as an exploration - a probe into some space that you realize you don't fully understand. Don't just throw it at a researcher. Use it to try something out. Make a bet.

Realize, and communicate to everyone over and over, that this is different from starting a new program. And it won't do everything everyone wants. But we can't count on someone else to give us an easy answer. So we're going to send out a probe.

This is the most important part--and it's the piece that will require the deepest change from how we usually work (God knows we've all been stuck with Pilot Projects before):

1. **The results of the Little Bet have to undergo a clear-eyed evaluation.** What worked, what didn't work, what did we learn. And most importantly, What Do We Still Not Know. In an economic development strategic planning training that I did recently, I pushed hard at the fact that no one wants to be evaluated. But we know why we have to. So we have to put on our big kid pants and just do it. Among all those professionals, no one said no.

2. **The results of the Little Bet have to be shared**...with your community, yes. But also with your neighbor communities, your region, other places that grapple with the same issues that you do.

   That's not just being nice, that's selfish self-interest. You will never, ever put together enough office supply budget to do all the Little Bets your community needs. You're going to have to get serious about sharing your results, so that others share their Little Bets with you too, so that you don't have to do them all yourself. Scientists build their experiments based on the findings of others, and they share their information transparently.

   Our methods in the community world may be too disjointed, too catch-as-catch-can at this point to do that research-sharing as well as the scientists do. Which probably helps explain why what they know has changed faster than what we do. We may need better systems for sharing our Little Bets. But we can at least start with the organizations we have. The key, though, will be to differentiate clearly between the Little Bets and the Our Successful Programs...and especially between the Little Bets and the Look How Great We Are In My Town stories. Both of those can be useful, but not in the same way the experimental notes from Little Bets would be.

3. **Change. Expect change. Assume change.** We have a hell of a time killing programs, usually because someone has a deep stake in it. Someone has benefited from it, invested in it, cares about it...has come to rely on it. Little Bets have to be presented and understood from the start as a learning tool, as a probe. From whatever works, from whatever we learn from it, something will grow from it. But this is not a Program. It's a probe. It's not permanent.

—

At this point in our community history, we're 500 miles from the North Pole, and we have to be honest and admit that we have absolutely no idea what to expect. But we know that we have to go there, and do it in a way that helps us learn.

No one else is going to hand us a map. All we can do is load up our dog sleds. And learn from each other.

Part 2, Implication 2:

Use Your Usability

Usability.

I'll explain where that weird word comes from in a minute. But here's the toe-in-the-water version:

Even the most messed-up places, the most pathetic, the most boring, the most abused by the law of unintended consequences, have assets. Something great about them. Or at least interesting. Something special, at least kind of special.

Something we might entirely overlook, or take for granted, or just see as a part of the landscape, not an asset that's actually worth anything. Something the economic developers probably didn't see as a feature worth putting on the web site, or to highlight in the video about our 8,000 acres of available industrial land and "great work ethic."

Economically valuable community assets often include things we're not used to thinking of as assets. Assets can be **people** - groups of people and their characteristics, like their experience building things or creating novel solutions or providing services to a certain kind of operation. Assets can be people we probably overlooked in the past, like young urban kids adept with new technology or immigrant neighborhoods with unique but unassuming restaurants. Assets can be **places**, like parks, waterfronts, downtowns, reasonably priced condos, Norman Rockwell neighborhoods. Assets can be **business expertise**, rate of volunteer involvement, community theater, access to assets that don't lie within your boundaries.

Assets make your community unique. They're what give your ecosystem the opportunities that don't place you in direct competition with Everyplace Else. They're what make you valuable to the people who want what you can offer. They're what give you the best chance out there to attract your own little slice of Talent. And they're the raw materials of getting yourself out of the Conventional Economic Development Race to the Bottom.

So see usability. And build on usability. This section will start to explore how.

I see usability

That was my dad's favorite saying. Dad had no hesitation about pulling things off the curb in front of the neighbors' houses. But he wasn't looking for salvage or a quick couple of dollars. He was looking for usability.

You'd probably call Dad a tinkerer. He always had projects in process – a car (or three) in various stages of disassembly on their way to being restored, an electronic gadget he insisted would work again if he could just find the loose wire, an idea for making something from the extra tin cans he brought home from the factory or the brass-plated fittings that a friend at the foundry gave him or the pile of tire irons he found on garbage day around the corner.

When I grew up and went home to visit, I knew he would want my undivided attention as he showed me his latest finds and played out his new ideas for making flower pots or bird feeders or paint brush holders or whatever.

One of my strongest memories: he would pull himself up to full (not very tall) height, puff out his (very slight) chest, hold up what looked like a random piece of junk, and declare:

"I...see...usability."

I'd nod and smile, but I didn't see it. And even when he did complete something (which didn't always happen), I failed to see the achievement in it (these weren't great works of art by any stretch).

But he never said he was going for artistry. He saw usability.

Maybe this is why my dad, who never finished college, understood the value of old places long before I did. Growing up in the small town where he also had gone to high school, the buildings and houses all around me seemed...tired. I knew that my friends who lived in the newer neighborhoods had whole house air conditioning, heat ducts instead of the metal radiator in my room that clunked and hissed but seldom seemed to heat anything, and walls that didn't require tedious, unending paint scraping every damn summer.

I did eventually turn into a historic preservation specialist during the 90s - I have the distinction of being responsible for listing some of the ugliest buildings on the National Register of Historic Places. In northern Wisconsin at that time, preservation mostly mattered to a few... well, the common perception was, crackpots. As late as the early 1990s, Green Bay still had a 1960s –era blight removal plan that identified most old downtown buildings for demolition as soon as the city could get them. I crawled through the basement of one of the final ones, documenting its last days, before it was demolished. I still have those photos.

Green Bay at that time was just starting to understand the economic benefits of preservation – but Dad understood entirely. He started to mail me clippings from the Cleveland papers (remember actual clippings?). And when I got on the phone with him, he was more excited to talk about a building or bridge rehab that he had read about than about what he and Mom were doing.

About nine months before my second son was born, Dad was diagnosed with a brain tumor. My last time with him was about a month before the baby was due – last time I could travel from Cincinnati, where we had moved, to Cleveland, a drive of about 3½ hours. Shortly before I left to go home, Dad sat me on the couch and pulled out a large envelope full of clippings. By this point, the cancer in the speech center of his brain was wreaking havoc on his ability to read or write, and my name on the outside of the envelope was spelled with three L's.

We spent a long time going through those clippings – all sorts of building rehabs and downtown revitalization stories in Cleveland and South Carolina and places that I had never heard of. And at one point, he looked at me directly, and told me that he was proud of me, that what I was doing was important.

This at a time when I doubted whether I could keep working, with a toddler at home and a baby on the way, when the cultural pressure to hang it up seemed to roar constantly in my ears.

These places matter. What you're doing to help them matters.

I see usability.

Dad died a week after Jonathan was born. We gave Jon his name because that was one of five that Dad had proposed when we asked him..

—

After all these years, and all this reading and listening and talking, I still don't fully understand why places, and particularly old places, matter to us – obviously there's the sense of history, the fact that these are often places that are built at the human scale and are thus more comfortable for us, the solid-ness of the materials, so on and so on.

But why do they matter so much, and on such a primal level?

Maybe it's because even the most run-down, aesthetically unpleasing places have usability. They so often have the potential to be so much more than they are. And that is where their greatest value, emotionally and economically, lies.

The rest of this section explores some of the factors that can inform our thinking about our places, to help us re-discover and reclaim our places' usability. And to find within that our best potential for economic sustainability.

I think Dad would like that.

Making room for What We Will Be Next

Damn movie. There's another one on the list.

I learned a long time ago that I am way too good at buying into what theater people call the willing suspension of disbelief – what you do when you get caught up in an acted-out story and react to it as though it were real, even when you know darn well that it's make believe. I have a ridiculously long list of movies that hit me so hard when I watched them, got me so worked up, that I know I can never watch them again. *What Dreams May Come?* Forget it. *The Mission?* No freakin way. *Up?* It's a cartoon, after all... crap.

I knew the first time I watched *Up* that I needed to skip the first five minutes about the main character's life with his wife and his losing her after a long happy marriage. Bull's eye on Pressure Point #1, but we can handle this.

Of course, near the end of the movie, that character has to re-confront his loss, accept it and let go. I walked in on my 10-year old son watching it last night (I had purposely avoided the room all evening, but it was getting late and I wanted him to go to bed), and ended up watching the last five minutes with him. Cue the waterworks.

In his book *The Great Reset,* Richard Florida writes most eloquently about the underlying sense of loss and struggle to move on that pervades many communities, particularly in the Rust Belt and other areas that have struggled to transition to the new economic epoch that is unfolding. As I have mentioned here before, many of the places I know best have been struggling to deal with that loss, and make that transition, for decades. We watched our parents come face to face with the consequences of a changing world long before we ever heard of Lehman Brothers.

Florida includes a lovely quote from John Craig, former editor of the *Pittsburgh Post-Gazette*:

> Fundamental change will be much longer in coming than you can imagine. You'll survive. But there'll be no 'getting over' your past, only moving beyond it. [12]

You also can't get back your past, as much as you might want it. It just doesn't work.

I have spent more time than I can count with communities where leaders – council members, Chamber of Commerce officials, and others – have said to me with complete sincerity, "we just need to get the shoe factory back." Or, a slightly more sophisticated approach to the same idea: "We just need to land another big factory/a new shopping mall/a new...something."

Go find that unicorn, and when we bring it back to our community, we will all live happily ever after.

—

We who work with communities know, or should know by now, that this is a fantasy. The world has changed, and is changing. We have to get on with it.

The psychologist Elizabeth Kubler-Ross described grieving as a five-step process: denial, anger, bargaining, depression, and finally, acceptance. In *Up,* the main character reaches the point of acceptance when the house in which he lived so happily with his wife, and which he

---

[12] Richard Florida, *The Great Reset: How New Ways of Living and Working Drive Post-Crash Prosperity.* HarperCollins e-books, p. 81 .

has clung to and protected throughout the movie, floats away into the distance (If you haven't seen it, trust me on that one. It involves a lot of balloons.)

For some of us, the greatest challenge we face is to help our communities allow their past identities – industrial heart, shopping mecca, favorite tony suburb-- float away.   In the community context, that requires a combination of

- Data that puts the change and the opportunity in front of our eyes,

> For some of us, the greatest challenge we face is to help our communities allow their past identities – industrial heart, shopping mecca, favorite tony suburb-- float away.

- An empathetic, collaborative approach that makes everyone, not just a few, the owners of our future, and

- A clear-eyed, pragmatic strategy for doing the tough, long-term work that has to happen to make that transition happen.

Florida also paraphrases and then quotes Howard Fineman of *Newsweek:*

> [The lesson of resurgent places] is to pick yourself up and get back to work. Don't expect the federal government or anyone else to save your city or bring back your industries. 'It is that the old world will inevitably disappear, and that creating a new one is up to you, not someone else.'[13]

---

[13] *Ibid.*

We have to remember, honor and love our pasts, but not cling to them. That's true for us as people and us as communities. Our current usability may be different from what it used to be. But we won't find out until we stop trying to recapture the past.

Only when we can help our communities do that work of letting go do we allow ourselves to have space for What We Will Be Next.

Everyone is Special... Really?

> In the end, I don't want a business here because we gave them the best deal - I want them here because they share our beliefs. If a business is here because they share our beliefs, I bet they will stay here and be more invested in our community than the company that came here just because they got the best deal.
>
> —William Lutz, "Economic Development: Does your place matter?"
> (wiseeconomy.com)

———

Meaningful investment, whether in the person you date, the phone you buy, or the community you choose for your business or your home, is usually based on something deeper than a straight cost-benefit analysis. Real commitment requires that we find a resonance, some sort of sympathetic vibration between who we are and what we value and what we understand of the other.

In economic development, there's a tendency to pooh-pooh that kind of talk. It's a flaky planner thing, like that mush mouthed vision they put in the comprehensive plan that no one reads.

What do businesses want, you ask? Oh, easy.

Low taxes. Big incentives. Access to 75% of the nation's population within a 600 mile radius.

What's the likelihood that you can really compete on low taxes and access to the same blob of population as every other city within 60 miles?

How does *that* make you special?

This is an old industrial-era economic development paradigm. It assumes that everyone shopping for a business location just showed up at Wal-Mart: we are looking at a shelf of indistinguishable gadgets, rows upon rows of detergent or paper towels, each with some different buzzword or bright package or stupid bear on the wrapper than has nothing to do with what the thing is supposed to do. We need one, so we grab one – maybe the one we've used in the past, maybe the one Uncle Joe works for, maybe the cheapest or the biggest. But most of the time, it's a purchase without loyalty. It's functional. It's the one we pick because it takes the least effort. Whatever.

But what's the likelihood that we'll make any effort on behalf of this purchase? Will we make a special trip to a different store if they stop carrying that brand? If they change the formula and it doesn't work as well with my tap water, will I storm the stockholder's meeting to insist that they change it back?

Nah, I got other things to do. I'll just grab something else.

Consumer brands spend literally billions of dollars per year to try to build loyalty to a one-dimensional, interchangeable, disposable thing. We see how well that works.

———

We who work with communities live in a world of the fascinating, the unique, the irreplaceable. That's what your mix of people, places, history, culture, economics, etc. gives you. The aspects that make you unique makes you *valuable* – whether you're a detergent that really does make whites whiter and brights brighter, or a community with a unique character and a unique place in the world

197

> We who work with communities live in a world of the fascinating, the unique, the irreplaceable. That's what your mix of people, places, history, culture, economics, etc. gives you.

that can provide something of value to a specific type of person or business. Specifically, people who are seeking a place that will give them that resonance.

Why on earth would we settle for being just another of the hundreds of places that has sites, a handful of incentives, a great "work ethic" (whatever that is), and access to some undifferentiated mass of people that are irrelevant to the vast majority of businesses? Blah blah blah. But we often do.

And we try to compensate by cranking on one of those levers on the economic development machine: we throw money at 'em. After all, the only way to stand out from the competition is the way Wal-Mart does: make yourself cheaper, and cheaper, and cheaper than everyone else.

Welcome to the Race to the Bottom.

Why not claim who we are, what we value, what we want to be.... Put that message out there, start exerting a pull on the people and businesses who might actually want *us*, not just the cheap inducements we offer?

Then, our places matter. Then there's a reason for people and businesses to have loyalty, to care what the hell happens here.

Then we have a chance to make a difference.

You're an old horse and wagon on Mulberry Street, and that's fine.

The Dr. Seuss book _And to Think That I Saw It on Mulberry Street_ was one of my kids' favorites when they were younger, and oddly enough, it's one of his oldest. In the story, a young boy anticipates that when he gets home from school, his dad will want him to describe what he saw on that walk. The boy, of course, has an urge to embroider the story, to make it more interesting, but he knows that will not go over well. So, as he thinks about what to tell his father, he agonizes over the fact that the only thing he saw on the way home was an old draft horse pulling an old wagon.

Not interesting enough. So he starts embellishing... just a little, and then a little more, until what he's going to describe goes from something the boy thinks is pretty boring to an impossible picture loaded with racing elephants and giraffes, exotic people, Seussian vehicles and an assortment of colorful chaos.

And of course, when the kid gets home ready to tell this wild story, he catches himself and tells the truth.

Here's the funny part: my kids loved the way the story goes wildly out of control, but they could never figure out why a horse pulling a wagon on a city street wasn't interesting enough to report by itself. They had a different context: if they saw a horse pulling a wagon on a street on the way home, that would of course be a very big deal.
On the other hand, the parade does include an (unnervingly stereotypical, but the book was published in 1937) Chinese person using chopsticks. My kids have watched their mother and father "eat with sticks" since they were tiny, so they never understood why that was in the parade.

What was unique and exotic to Dr. Seuss and his character was utterly blasé to my kids, and what was exotic to my kids was a routine part of life for the author when he wrote the book in the 1930s. In this case, that's a factor of the time difference between the writing and the reading, but what I want you to notice is how differently different people perceived the same environment.

In a previous section I pulled out an old trick of mine: the comparison of a certain location's native flower to one that's much more exotic. In that case, it was an apple tree blossom and a hibiscus. The point in that comparison is that the native flower is much easier to grow in that environment. If the point is to produce blossoms as efficiently as possible, with as little special treatment or fussing as possible, the native plant will beat the exotic almost all the time (when it doesn't, we have a kudzu-weed type problem, but that's another metaphor for another day).

The horse and wagon on Mulberry Street story puts another twist on the native/exotic issue: what is routine from one perspective is crazy amazing for another. A person eating with chopsticks is not anything I would give a second glance. But a horse and wagon trundling down the street in front of my window would definitely get my attention.

The auxiliary of that point is that your community will *not* be unique, and therefore more valuable, to everyone. If I am not interested in horses and wagons, or chopsticks or low water rates or warehouse space or mountain climbing, and that is what makes your community unique, I am not going to consider your community more valuable than anywhere else.

But someone else, someone who wants those amenities, will. And since that someone else will regard your community as having more value, as being worth more, there's no point in wasting the limited resources you have chasing me, when you could be putting your effort into chasing him or her.

That means that we have to do three things well:

1. **We need to understand very clearly what makes our community unique.** That's not just something we can pull out of the air, out of our usual assumptions and our portfolio of past ad campaigns. That's something that we need to analyze, put together data about, make sense of. Maybe more importantly, we have to make sure that we are seeing the community the way an outsider without our emotional baggage and history will. You can do that, but it requires a very strong emphasis on the outside perspective. And most importantly, it *must* be true.

2. **We need to articulate what makes us unique - and articulate it not just once, not just through the channels that we are used to using, but as broadly and consistently as possible.** Once isn't enough. Once is an anomaly to the reader or listener - a novelty, not a compelling argument. That doesn't mean that we have to flog the same story, the same three talking points, over and over. It does mean that our understanding of what makes us unique must include a variety of threads that together create a compelling image. It's our job to weave those threads together for the reader or listener, and that will take a sustained effort, not just a weeklong Facebook push.

3. **We need to target what we do and what we offer.** The glossy ad in *Business Week* with the

aerial view of your industrial park has long since outlived its usefulness, if it was ever effective to begin with. Instead, we need to find ways to get our message to the people that are most likely to value what makes us unique. It's not difficult and it's not costly. But it does take time and concerted effort.

Part 2, Implication 3:

The Real Power of Small Businesses

A short list of the premises that I have attempted to lay out so far in this book (after you sort through the cars and lemonade and what all) would include:

- Local economies are ecosystems, and need to be managed as such,

- Talent rules, and talent is scarce,

- You can't sell your way to a better community.

- Your existing assets equal your best opportunities

- The stuff you can do that will most effectively strengthen your economic ecosystem isn't exciting or flashy, but it's the stuff that will matter most.

One issue where all of this comes together, and where people who care about economic development needs to substantially refocus our efforts, is on growing our communities' small business ecosystems.

Like I said earlier, I am not going to tell you that "Small Businesses are *Awesome!!!!* They can fix *Everything!!!!*" But given that the average business size, across the board, is shrinking fast, and the very nature of working for someone is coming unpinned from the someone we used to work for, we need to take a deep look at how we can enable all of the small business sectors of our ecosystem, from the tech start-ups to the strip mall retailers, to strengthen their capacity and generally live up to their potential.

The next few sections will focus on that.

Nope, not that.

"Entrepreneurs will solve *everything*!!!! Yay yay yay!!!"

If you read books about startups, or you've heard a few common conference speakers, you might have heard this.

It won't.

Pretending that we can return to the world of medieval shopsmiths, or Andy Griffith-style small towns, is exactly that: pretending. We live in a hyper-interconnected, choice-laden, preference-swarming world. If the locally-owned shoe store doesn't carry my (very small) size, I don't have to settle for the brogans my grandma would wear because that's the only option available. I can go 10 other places in nearby towns, or more likely, online, to pick exactly the kind of platform wedge with the squared toe that I was looking for. Pretending that I can or will buy everything I need or want from the local guys makes for a nice happy picture, but it's not going to be reality.

Retail is the easy example to think about, but that's true for manufacturers, tech providers, pretty much everyone else. We cannot realistically expect our people to shift all their economic habits to our little village. It doesn't work that way anymore.

Given that, though, shifting a significant portion of our community resilience efforts to small business feeding and development makes a ton of sense, again for very pragmatic reasons:

- **Small businesses are growing** in number, economic reach and economic impact. Pragmatically, in sheer numbers, the businesses we're dealing with, more and more, are small.

- **Small businesses are getting smaller**, often micro-smaller. That means that not only are there a whole hell of a lot more of them to deal with, but they're operating with less and less of their own internal capacity. That's a huge and growing problem, because it raises their risk of imploding. Which is not just about them, but a risk to your community as well.

- **Small businesses, on the whole, are better equipped to pivot** — to change their products, their operations, their sales methods, etc. when changes in technology or consumer tastes or transportation threaten to leave their work in the dust. As economic and technological and everything else change continues to accelerate, small businesses will be able to tack away from the storms, while the big businesses risk swamping in the waves.

Small businesses are not just mini versions of the big guys. Whether you're dealing with tech startups, doctors' offices or fast casual pizza, small businesses function in ways that are fundamentally different from big operations in the same field. That means that they might not really need what you've been offering. That means that they probably most need something else.

Lashing Together

"We businesses need [economic development] organizations. We need them to help every segment of the community to succeed. We need the economy to have multiple legs. Economic development should ask: what I can do to help businesses lash up with others?"

-James E Jardon, II, CEO JHT Incorporated and Medical Curriculum Technologies. Opening Keynote, 2013 Leadership Conference, International Economic Development Council.

When boats lash up, they tie up to each other broadside (long edge of the hull). Usually you do that so that people can move from one boat to another easily, like you might want to do if you're having a party. It's easier to share the burgers and the wine bottles among your friends if your boats are lashed together.

But the other reason you might lash together is to help weather a storm. If your boat is anchored alone, you only have one or two points holding you down, but if you lash to other boats that have also dropped anchors, then you have much better odds of staying out in the deep and not getting blown into shore.

We started this book by talking about a local economy as an ecosystem to be managed, rather than a machine to be unsuccessfully manipulated. And we continued by talking about finding usability - the idea that your place will have the most value for those who want what it uniquely has to offer. The benefit of an ecosystem, and a place that builds on its usability, is its resilience – it's ability to weather the storm because of its connections. So let's explore how that works.

Small Business Ecosystem

From my point of view, the long-term benefits of growing a robust small business economy are pretty clear:

- A small business-based economy is more resilient, on the whole, than one that depends on a single business or a small number or large enterprises. Don't believe me? Let me time travel you to Cleveland in the 1970s...or Las Vegas in 2007, or Detroit in 2008. Local economies that depend on one industry experience brutally hard crashes.

- A small business-based economy has more ability to adapt to changing markets because it's easier to change course for a small business than a larger one.

- A small business-based economy may arguably provide more opportunities for employment growth than one loaded with large industries. Google "job creation and small business" and you will get Bureau of Labor statistics about job creation trends among large and small businesses. This isn't a new phenomenon; the story has been the same for a couple of decades.

- When some of your small businesses do one day grow into large businesses, you'll probably find that they are more likely to stay put, and become contributing corporate citizens, than something you cajoled into coming to town with a hefty incentive. That's not a guarantee, but it does increase your odds.

Important stuff. You would think that growing this sector of the economy would be where we would logically put our effort, rather than leaving it to chance. But so often, we don't.

Small businesses in most communities face incredibly steep odds to success. Most don't have enough resources – of any type. Pick one. Loans are hard to come by, start-up funds are slim, markets untested, staff expensive. Uncertainty runs rampant. And if the potential business operator is not white, or blessed with wealthy relatives, or otherwise privileged, then the odds stack even higher.

Even successful small businesses face a constant string of trials. How do you manage employees and payroll? How do you keep inventory from drowning you in costs? How do you navigate local government regulatory systems? How do you retire without losing the value you have built up over the years?

The biggest barriers almost always come down to capacity, define that however you like. When my dad was Vice President of the little paint factory, his duties included the following:

- Keeping the alcoholic shipping clerk on the job,
- Purchasing and storing toxic chemicals,
- Re-working the books when he discovered that my grandfather (the company president) had been skimming profits, and
- Dragging into the shop on Cleveland February midnights to try to cajole the ancient boiler into functioning for one more day.

Don't know how to fix a boiler? Don't know how to keep a troubled employee working?

No small business owner knows how to do it all, or has time and money to get an expert. But they try to do it all anyways, the best they can.

—

So, it comes down to capacity. What can a community do to give its small businesses the best chances to succeed?

When you grow a garden, you don't build the plants out of rocks and plastic. You create the environment where those tiny, threadlike little seedlings have the best chance you can give them of growing into strong and resilient plants. Some plants grow faster than others, some are inherently hardier. You can't do it for them. Your job is to give them the best chance you can give them to grow.

Interdependence

Small businesses most differ from larger businesses because of the repercussions of their limited capacity (capacity for management, bookkeeping, marketing, anything involving a need for human time). Small businesses, regardless of industry, need to be able to supplement their limited capacity by being able to reach out for help when they need it.

Here's two simple examples – one a business, one not (well, not entirely). Let's take the second one first.

My husband broke his shoulder blade when he wrecked his bicycle on a trail last year. He messed it up pretty good – fractured in two places and partially out of joint (I told him that the front-double-somersault-over-the-handle-bars dismount was best left to the professionals, but sometimes they don't listen).

The weeks after that for me, from a work and a home front standpoint, got pretty garbled. I entered a period of Things are Not Getting Done... whether it was that presentation that I have *got* to get written, or attending my son's school open house. We just couldn't keep all the balls in the air with three functional adult arms and one out of two brains trying to fall asleep from the medications all the time.

If we had had family in town that could manage some of the kid logistics, or if this presentation was of a type that I could hand off to someone else, we could have tackled everything, or at least more of it. If we had had a higher level of *interdependence*, we would have had more access to *capacity* at the moment when we needed it.

The issue isn't money, entirely, or time, entirely. It's capacity, and particularly flexible, available- when-needed capacity. And for about two months, neither the Wise Economy Workshop nor the Rucker household had anywhere near enough of it.

> If we had had a higher level of *interdependence*, we would have had more access to *capacity* at the moment when we needed it.

One day during that period, I spent a couple of hours trying to work from a coffee shop a few minutes away (it was patient nap time and I didn't want to risk waking him). I've been there many times, and as far as I can tell, the only person who works there is the owner.

Think about that for a minute. If you are trying to run a coffee shop without employees, what do you do when there is a delivery at the back door? When do you clean the bathroom (when do you use the bathroom, for that matter)? Perhaps he gets the Subway employees at the end of the block to accept his deliveries when he is busy, or perhaps he pays someone to clean the place or balance his books after he closes. I don't really know.

Here's the tough part, though, if you're in his shoes:

How much of your total personal capacity does the business consume, and how do you deal with the fact that you can't do everything? And what happens when the well of your personal capacity runs dry?

This, in a nutshell, is the real reason why a healthy small business ecosystem needs to foster interdependence: small businesses need to be able to draw on others to supplement their own capacity, especially in a flexible way that enables them to get that when they need it without carrying an unsustainable and not-always-needed cost on their backs.

———

That all sounds nice and happy.

But there's one more piece to that interdependence: in a healthy small business ecosystem, people understand that others' success or failure will directly impact their own thriving or struggling. When it flourishes, that awareness that leads to a strengthened sense of responsibility to and for the community. And that's an ethos that we as a culture often haven't done much to build up.

Small business owners, understandably, tend to think of themselves as *independent* - "I built this business, it's mine, I am king of my castle, *don't you mess with me.*"

That's all fine and good when you work on a 3,000-acre spread, miles from anyone else. For the typical small business, that's a dangerous stance– for themselves and for others.

Here's an easy visual: picture the stereotypical downtown eyesore owned by the 79-year old guy with the pawn shop that hasn't had its front window washed since Eisenhower was president. Not only is he not doing himself any favors, but he's probably having a negative impact on the businesses and property owners around him.

Again, that's an overly easy example, but you can sing the same tune with a lot of different words.

In a healthy small business ecosystem, owners and managers understand that, like it or not, they are to at least some extent interdependent on other businesses in their district or cluster. The degree and type of interdependence varies depending on the type of business activity, the type of business space, whether or not customers see the location, how spread out they are physically, etc. But to be optimally successful, a small business cannot pretend that it is an island unto itself.

> To be optimally successful, a small business cannot pretend that it is an island unto itself.

Cowboys don't work in storefronts or warehouses or office cubicles – and small businesses need neighbors who understand that they all are, will you or won't you, in this together.

In a lot of cases, like my pawn shop owner, our small businesses have forgotten that part. And they need some help remembering.

Building (or re-building) interdependence takes hard work. It takes consistent communication, illuminating those interdependencies, probably pointing them out to some individuals over and over. And it takes the sometimes-unpleasant work of challenging assumptions and changing how people think about the environment in which they operate. It's work that takes time. It's work that takes grit. But it's the right work. It's building that healthy small business ecosystem.

MOAR Gardens!

When you grow a garden, you don't build the plants out of rocks and plastic. You create the environment where those tiny, threadlike little seedlings have the best chance you can give them of growing into strong and resilient plants. Some plants grow faster than others, some are inherently hardier. You can't do it for them. Your job is to give them the best chance you can give them to grow.

Just like gardeners work at giving their plants the best odds to thrive, we who care about communities can build an environment where our small businesses have the best chances to grow.

-Me, a couple of sections ago.

Fine. Enough with the damn garden. You can't build seedlings out of rocks and plastic. Got it.

What the hell are we supposed to do?

There's lots of experts on small business - and thousands of variants of "How to Run Your Small Business" books geared to everyone from landscape contractors to nanotech inventors. You don't have to become the expert on Everything You Never Wanted to Know About A Small Business And Didn't Know You Should Ask. Your biggest potential impact is probably your ability to help small businesses lash up to the whole range of resources your community has to offer.

And since you're already in the gardening business, we might as well torture the metaphor a little further:

- **Help potential entrepreneurs select the right seeds.** Small business owners sometimes jump in with a stunning lack of market knowledge. Entrepreneurs tend to start businesses on a gut sense of an

216

opportunity – or on a "gee, it would be cool to do that" sort of model. A lot of times that works out just fine — often they can find opportunities that will never show up on the site selectors' reports. But those entrepreneurs also face a huge risk of wrong moves or mistaken choices — and the biggest risk of wrong choices is that they cut into a small business's limited capacity. Missteps in the beginning can set a business up for failure, and anything that wastes capacity cuts away at a very thin layer of reserves.

Communities can help new businesses select the right seeds by sharing real-world information about their assets and their opportunities. What's our economic makeup? Where are we over-supplied or undersupplied? What are the hidden, maybe small-scale opportunities that result from population subsets or unusual regional destinations that out-of-towners might not know about? This information isn't hard to come by, if you know where to look. But it can make all the difference between a hometown success story and a could-have-been-if-only.

- **Preparing the soil.** If you are starting a garden on a vacant lot, you don't just throw seeds down and hope for the best. You have to make sure that the dirt can nourish the plants you're planning to grow, and of course all dirt is certainly not created equal. What you need to add or do depends on what you are planning to grow. Peat moss? Mulch? Compost? Fertilizer? Lime? One seed needs one, one seed needs another.

Some business types benefit from opportunities to build strong local networks, while others need international connections. Sometimes they need help with inventory management, human relations issues, finding funding to grow into their potential. None of these require a degree in rocket science, but again, remember capacity:

If I am an overwhelmed small business owner, chances are I will stumble along by the seat of my pants — until the crisis that has been building up takes front and center. By then, it may be too late.

If we want to build a small business ecosystem, one of the easiest and simplest things we can do is to make this assistance easily available. Chances are someone somewhere is providing the information your local business needs... your businesses just aren't aware of it or able to get it with what little energy they have to throw at it. Putting that within reach isn't hard...but it takes consistent effort and lots of repetition. Just like with fertilizing, once is never enough.

- **Monitoring the ecosystem's development.** Biologists don't just look at an ecosystem once – they identify key measurable indicators, and they check them regularly. What's the water pH? How many songbirds did we count this year? Are we above or below the average for rainfall? How else are you going to understand where things are going – or what we need to change in order to nudge trends in a better direction?

We do a particularly lousy job of monitoring our local small business ecosystems. We tend to assume that everything is fine based on a few overly-simplistic indicators, like the number of new businesses, without digging deeper into the data to understand whether those factors are actually signs of growth or decline. An increase in the number of birds might look like a good sign to a biologist, but if most of the growth is invasive species who compete with the natives, that numerical increase might not be such a good thing. Similarly, adding jobs that pay minimum wage or require only minimal skills could be less something to crow about than something to take as a warning signal.

None of these tasks are hard, and none of them require skills or information that we don't already have or can borrow from other professions. What we do need to bring to it is the diligence and the long-term perspective to cultivate our small business ecosystems. It won't happen overnight.

How easy it is to run a small business that sucks

It's incredibly, stunningly easy to run a small business that sucks.

One of the side effects of the implosion of the retail real estate market in many places is that the amount of really cheap space in many locations has skyrocketed. If you have a business idea, and a little cash on hand, chances are you can find some property owner with a paid-off mortgage who will rent you that storefront or warehouse for a song. And as we increasingly idolize entrepreneurs, and as we keep telling people that going into business for yourself holds the promise of happy prosperity, more and more people will take us up on that offer.

Including a lot of people who have no damn business running a business.

Small business owners, over and over again, remind me of movie cowboys: tough, independent, self-sufficient, needing nothing from nobody. Behind that façade though, a lot of those entrepreneurs face each day overwhelmed, struggling to muster from within just themselves the full range of skills and resources that they need to run a successful business.

The good ones know that. But many small business owners have no idea what they don't know.

It's easy for us to just write off business success or failure as the machine of "the market" doing its supposedly impartial work. But like anything else, it's not that simple. Places - whether storefronts or whole cities - can get a reputation as a lousy business place pretty quickly, even when we can see great potential. It only takes a couple of wanna-be entrepreneurs getting a sweetheart deal from a desperate or disinterested property owner, and then crashing in flames when they botch their hiring or their inventory or their marketing, for that "bad spot" reputation to develop. And for independent businesses, more likely to rely on experience and gut check than the data that the franchises devour, reputation becomes a very solid reality.

Here's where you and your community's revivified economic development come in. You can help them lash up - to the information they need and the other businesses of their community.

If you're not linking your small business owners to detailed, hands-on training and coaching, you're shooting your community in the foot. If you're not inducing or requiring your incentive recipients to go through intensive business training, you're wasting too much of your limited funding. And if you're not helping your local businesses find, learn about and learn to buy and sell from each other, you're missing a powerful piece of firepower in your campaign to strengthen the resilience of your local economy. And if increasing business growth in historically overlooked communities and populations matters to you, then you need to pay more attention to these issues than anyone else.

Here's perhaps the most important point: you need to have some process, some system, that will help some of your potential small business owners learn the most valuable thing they may ever learn:

That opening that business would be a bad idea.

Sometimes the best thing you can do to help manage your community's ecosystem is to keep the unhealthy ones from getting planted in the first place.

Pedestrian Scale Economies

Bad planner confession: if I hear one more person talk about "walkability," I'm going to throw up.

Just like anyone else, planners can get obsessive about some new, cool idea and start promoting that as the magic bullet, the Grand Answer to Everything. There's a school of thought among planners these days that promises that "walkable" design is the answer to all community ills. Increase density, install sidewalks and bike paths, get rid of the big wide streets and All Will Be Great. Their professional grandfathers insisted that we needed to separate cars from people, now, to some extent, the opposite holds court.

But like many easy binary choices, there's a grain of truth in here - one that people focused on local economies should grasp:

What the planners are discovering is that people, no matter their gender or race or income, do seem to like walkable spaces. They pick them over places built for cars, more than nine times out of ten. As Peter Calthorpe and others have shown, even the fiscal impacts work better in walkable environments.

There's a useful principle here that can migrate across to other issues that impact community vitality. Pedestrian environments seem to thrive because they provide:

- Lots of options,
- An easy-to-browse mix of those options,
- Consistent interesting-ness over time (even if one shop goes out, chances are there's enough other easy-to-access options to make it still worth a visit).

223

Proposition: we might have a better chance at long-term economic vitality, at resilience in the face of setbacks, if we quit looking for big wins and set as our priority a new goal: building a **pedestrian-friendly** *economy*. One that gives its residents lots of options for working and shopping and all that, one where all those options are clearly visible (not only to the diehard insiders who know where all the interesting but marginal backlot establishments are).

And perhaps most importantly, a local economy that can maintain its value over time, even as businesses come and go, because no one business dominates the economy.

What is work, anyways? 1099ers in your economy

Another big challenge when it comes to building small business ecosystems for resilient communities: the very nature of being employed looks nothing like we traditionally think it does. And that means that many of our well-intentioned efforts to support the growth of creative and innovation-based industries miss key opportunities to foster those sectors' growth.

In the U.S., we call many of these folks 1099ers (after the IRS form used to report their earnings), or freelancers or contract workers. Although rideshare drivers and delivery app workers have captured much of the recent national discussion and driven new awareness of this population, large numbers of 1099ers have professional, technical and/or creative skills that they use to provide services to a client under a contract. They might have one client or several dozen. They might spend their days on a computer, in a meeting, or in a workshop. They might work in splendid isolation or as part of a team. And while rideshare and delivery 1099ers have been well-documented as under-compensated and often denied the employment status and benefits that they may deserve, others choose 1099 status to preserve their independence, flexibility, and ability to use their skills as they see fit.

As early as 2012, the International Economic Development Council's *ED Now* journal asserted that as much as *one fifth* of the U.S. workforce may qualify as a

1099er.[14] And it appears likely that this number has increased since then.

Why is that so vague?

Simple: conventional economic data sources, like the Economic Census, don't count them. The way the analysis is set up, we simply cannot see them.

I am on my second gig as a 1099er (I had a different consulting business in the 1990s). My brother, the lady I had lunch with today, the guy in West Dayton I am working with and eight of the last 10 people I connected with on LinkedIn are 1099ers. So is my neighbor the illustrator, my neighbor the accountant, my friend's husband the IT professional, my colleague's husband the architectural designer, and...you get the idea. If you aren't looking for them, you might not see them. But we are everywhere – young, old, suburban, urban, stereotypically "creative" and boringly technical.

Welcome to the new small business ecosystem.

So what, some of you say. Freelancers are nothing new.

True, but here's the challenge: if more and more of our employment, and particularly our creative and technical employment (read: Talent), is working as 1099ers, what does that imply for local economic development, for those small business ecosystems that we need to foster?

There's been a lot written on this topic in terms of state and federal impacts on issues like healthcare and

---

[14] Erik R. Pages. "The Forgotten Fifth? Understanding and Supporting Your Community's Independent Workforce." Volume 11 / Number 3 / Summer 2012.

other conventional benefits. But I can find little analysis yet about how this trend impacts and will impact local communities. Obviously, state and federal policies on issues like health care and taxes have a big impact, but there's several key factors that we need to have on our radar when we look at how to grow healthy small business ecosystems in our local communities.

- **1099ers are like yogis in their flexibility**. I don't mean that they can twist into a pretzel (God knows I can barely bend my leg most days), but I do mean that their choices of how and where to apply their skills are pretty close to wide open. If I am a computer programmer, I have to decide whether to pursue government contracts, corporate gigs, develop my own products for sale or... do something else that most people don't know anything about. Or I can try to hedge my bets and pursue all of them, which might mean I don't pursue anything very effectively.

  Which approach is the best depends on a complex interplay between the market and my skill sets, and chances are there is no clear best path. On top of that, the best path for today might be a dead end tomorrow, so these folks have to maintain a constant ability to pivot.

  All of that is a whole lot easier said than done, and if the 1099ers in your local economy are spin-offs from a corporate setting, or young adults trying to get established, you're depending on them to make the right decisions on complicated issues that can easily determine whether they succeed or fail (not to mention whether they contribute to your local economy).

If 1099ers make up an important part of your local economic strategy, how smart is it to leave their choices entirely to chance?

- **1099ers work anywhere, and often many anywheres. And good anywheres are hard to find.** As I mentioned, I have been a 1099er for the majority of the last 20 years. A lot of times it seems like change is the only constant. Some weeks I work from home, some weeks I work from a workshare space or a back room in a client's office. Some weeks I seem to do my best work in a coffee shop, and some days I have to have silence. Some weeks I end up on an 8 to 6 work schedule, and some weeks (like the last week before the kids go back to school…ahem) it's catch as catch can.

All this has to do with that Third Places issue that some economic development people have picked up on from planners, but it also means much more.

Most of your 1099ers can't work in a coffee shop all the time – flexible arrangements for small office space can be unbelievably valuable, which is why coworking spaces have proliferated in many cities.[15] But one of the biggest spatial gaps that impacts 1099ers is meeting space. Some 1099ers can do everything online, but if you need to meet in person and put your heads together on a project, even a nice coffee shop

---

[15] Writing from the vantage point of early 2021, in the later phase of the COVID-19 pandemic, it's not at all clear to me what the coworking landscape is going to look like in the future. Although coworking facilities proliferated between 2013 and 2020, at this point you can make equally good arguments for their growth, or their demise, after this pandemic is over.

can be too much distraction and confusion for serious creative or problem-solving work.

In my entrepreneurial life, I have held meetings in library rooms, classrooms, borrowed company meeting room, rented spaces in coworking facilities, free spaces in coworking facilities, park benches, dining room tables, coffee shop storage rooms (that took some begging and a long time buying lattes), and who knows where else.

Inexpensive professional meeting space is the unicorn of the 1099er – and something most communities could provide easily.

- **Safety net? What safety net?** Passage of the Affordable Care Act in 2010 made 1099 employment much more possible for Americans of all walks of life, and has probably impacted the growth of 1099 employment as much as any other possible factor. As my brother, a longtime freelancer with a family that includes a special needs child once wrote, "ACA made it possible for us to function."

As I write this paragraph in 2021, health care reform continues to be a topic of ongoing debate, but it at least appears likely now that the major provisions of that law will stay in place. If there are attempts in your state to restrict health care access, I would strongly recommend that you fight to keep or expand it, because that will have a direct impact on whether or not you are able to keep your freelancers and equip them to grow. Research on small business growth led by the American Sustainable Business Council and others has documented the extent to which health care costs disadvantage small businesses by forcing them to choose between paying high costs out of their narrow profits, or losing the ability to retain high quality employees.

All of this doesn't mean that you have to get into the insurance business, but it also doesn't mean you can ignore it. It might be in the community's best interest to identify and promote resources that might help 1099ers get better insurance at a lower cost. Does a local or regional chamber offer small business insurance? Does your state permit collective insurance groups to organize?

You should also think more broadly about how to help bridge other gaps. Could a barter system help some of your 1099ers bridge the occasional tough gap? Can your organization support or sponsor mutual lending circles?

That last point comes back to perhaps the most important point in the transition from conventional economic development approaches to an emphasis on building a small business ecosystem: No one, even your government or agency, can do it alone. Our role has to shift from doer to mobilizer, from implementer to organizer – from project manager to team leader.

———

I use education analogies a lot, partly because that's a key element of my background, and partly because everyone's been a student.

When I talk about shifting our roles from implementer to organizer, what I am talking about is akin to what you learn when you become a teacher.

As a teacher, I could not *make* my students learn. I could not put the stuff they needed to know inside their heads. What I could do, and what I had to do if they were

230

going to learn anything, was create the environment and give them access to the tools that they needed to learn (and yes, sometimes the promise of unpleasant consequences comes in pretty handy).

As a result, the learning that the students get is never perfect, not as perfect as it would be if I could just dump the facts inside their heads. But it's the only result that is realistically achievable.

Our small business ecosystems in general, and our 1099ers in particular, need us to learn more closely from good teachers.

Part 2, Implication 4:

Don't waste your incentives

Most of these Implications have been pretty general, applicable to a large number of dimensions of the building a resilient community experience, But with this one, all of a sudden we land fairly solidly in the world of economic development policy.

There's a reason for that.

Economic development incentives aren't on a lot of the general public's agendas, but they're crucial to how the public sector component of our communities are accustomed to addressing economic challenges within a community. Incentives are used across everything from manufacturing to affordable housing developments, and they have an outsized impact on how our communities evolve, both physically and economically.

If our economic development incentives are pointed in the wrong direction, then our communities are like a boat dragging an anchor -- still moving in the direction that the wind and waves are pushing us, but at a lot slower speed than it should be. And often causing unintended consequences by tearing up the plants and ground beneath it.

But once the anchor is down, it takes effort to pull it back in and redeploy it in the right place; sometimes our organizations keep using our incentives the same way we have been. Because we aren't paying attention to whether their incentives are helping or dragging.

When I wrote the first version of this book, economic development incentives for new businesses had become a point of controversy, at least within the world of economic development professionals. The *New York Times'* massive study of incentives had just been released in September 2012, raising serious questions about the widespread practice of offering large amounts of money (directly or indirectly) to new businesses in a state or city. And at the 2013 International Economic Development Council's winter leadership conference, a very tense debate unfolded onstage between the lead author of that reporting and leaders of the professional organization. I finished the first version of this book about 6 months later.

What changed after that?

In some respects, a good deal has changed, The Foxconn development in southeastern Wisconsin, recipient of one of the largest incentive packages in history, turned into a political debacle for the state's Republican leadership in the late 2010s, as the company failed to deliver on the benchmarks it was supposed to reach and state and local agencies found themselves on the hook for extensive infrastructure (and eminent domain property acquisitions) for a project that at this writing looks like it may never come to fruition. Meanwhile, declining budgets and the evaporation of big manufacturing projects in many parts of the U.S. following the Great Recession meant that many states and cities found fewer opportunities to extend big incentive projects. And many repositioned their incentives programs to provide more support to existing local facilities that proposed to add or retain jobs or equipment. A few states, like Ohio, even created some incentive support for needs like employee upskilling, which would have seemed radical before 2013.

But in many ways, the incentives-offering site selection chase, although promising fewer big game trophies, accelerated. The Amazon H2 location search consumed the waking hours of economic development staff across the country for most of 2017, while the information Amazon released after the site selection was announced demonstrated that quality of workforce and workforce needs like housing played a much bigger role in Amazon's selection than the incentives offered did. Despite aggressive incentive packages from places as varied as Ottawa, Ontario and Tucson, Arizona, Amazon chose the two East Coast locations that promised the best possible access to talent, as well as to financial and political power: New York City and Washington, DC. Two locations that they would certainly have had on the top of their list regardless of the incentives.

And New York State's offering of a stunning $1.525 billion (yes, that's right) incentives package didn't keep the company there when a subset of politicians and residents protested.

So. Why do cities and states keep doing this at all?

––––

We don't know what new pressures will fall on these strategies as a result of the economics of the post-COVID-19 pandemic era, but it appears likely that the twin demands of cratered public funds and torn-up small and local businesses could result in a massive reallocation of what remains of those funds to regrowing strong small business ecosystems.

Or those who control those purse strings could get panicky and double down on throwing their funds at the few big recruitment opportunities that exist.

I'm rooting for the first option, and all of the Undercurrents and Implications I've noted in this book so far would seem to make that likely, at least in the longer term. But as I said in the introduction, I'm also a lot less confident in our ability to shift paradigms quickly today than I was in 2013. So I think it's still important for all of us, economic developers or not, to think very clearly about how to allocate our incentive funds in a manner that accelerates our growth into a resilient future, rather than letting incentives become an anchor that we drag.

Junk Food

I am beginning to think that economic development incentives are analogous to junk food for our communities. In the short term, they might satisfy our hunger and we might even feel better about ourselves and our community. But in the long run, the questions remain:

Is it worth it?

Will our communities continue to bloat up with empty buildings?

Could have the dollars that were used for incentives been better used elsewhere?

Was the easiest decision also the best?

—William Lutz. "Economic Development's Junk Food?" (wiseeconomy.com)

We have squawked too much about incentives over the past couple of years. A lot of times the "debate" has sounded more like chickens in a pen than reasoned discussion: yes-no-yes-no-yes-no.

The corn is bad. Eat the corn or you won't eat anything. Squawk, squawk, squawk.

I have it on good assurance that corn isn't all that a chicken will eat. And a chicken fed only on corn, like a kid fed only on corn dogs, is going to get very sick.

—

We have deep and substantial needs in communities and regions that are calling us to facilitate sea changes in economies, and in many cases our incentive policies do not move us in the direction of those goals. Or they might be doing that, but we don't know if they are, we don't have the right information to know what they're doing, and as a result we can't demonstrate whether they are doing what we need them to or not.

> We all got used to being able to just wing this – just assume that everything was working fine – when we had local economies that were flush enough to hide a little sloppiness, or some wishful thinking.

We all got used to being able to just wing this – just assume that everything was working fine – when we had local economies that were flush enough to hide a little sloppiness, or some wishful thinking, or over-simple assumptions about how we handled incentives. But now, with relief for budget pressures nowhere in sight, and with basics like how work *works* changing faster and faster, we don't have that slack anymore. There's just nowhere to hide.

I am not against incentives per se. I have spent much of my career working with downtowns and disadvantaged communities. A well-placed incentive can tip a place or a business sector from economically infeasible to economically possible, and when that happens it has direct and profound impacts on the people who live and work and invest in that community. But if an incentive isn't having that kind of impact, it's wasting money that we just don't have to waste anymore.

Incentive practices will eventually change because the forces on them are only getting stronger. The question in my mind is, how much of our limited resources will we waste with trying to hold back that tide? And how will our resistance affect the communities, and the people, who don't adapt, and who find themselves trying to swim in those waters?

The deep, and deeper, and deepest challenge.

Trying to craft a cogent and fair assessment of the incentives issue and the responsibilities of those of us who care about communities is feeling like the Gordian knot...you may never be able to lay the string out neat and pretty-like.

I don't think there's any question that the *principle* behind incentives, as a rule, has legitimacy, and that incentives can be important. When I served on the board of the Main Street program in Green Bay, we offered tiny little incentives -- a few hundred dollars for a new sign or a building facade improvement. And those incentives made a difference. They enabled improvements that benefited the business and the district, and they helped make those improvements happen at a time when most of these businesses could not get funding or could not convince landlords that it was worth it. Those incentives helped move the needle for the district. Those incentives mattered.

I also don't think there's any question that we often use incentives badly. Very badly. As many other commentators on economic development have pointed out, we waste a lot of money on incentives that, if we honestly went back and evaluated the results, didn't generate the payoffs we promised or were promised. Between the dozens of official reports and exposes that have been generated on the subject nationwide, there is too much of a preponderance of evidence on that point to come to any other general conclusion. Sometimes, like in the case of Rhode Island's 38 Studios fiasco, it's obvious quickly that the incentive was a bust. Many times, we don't understand how wasted the effort and the cost was until years later - if we are ever aware of it at all.

Here's where it starts getting tough:

Both the scope of problematic incentives in the U.S., and the fact that incentive programs are developed in a keeping-up-with-the-Jones, you-gotta-play-the-game mentality, indicates that the problem with incentives isn't incidental -- it's not simply a factor of some bureaucrats not doing their due diligence properly, or some short-sighted misunderstandings. It's across the board.

It's systemic. It's not a melanoma, confined to a few spots and relatively easy to remove. It's a leukemia, or a cancer that has metastasized.

That systemic problem is threatening the viability and resilience of both communities and the local government professions. Not just economic development, but planning and community development and administration and all the work and people who are tied into local development and funding. As local government and nonprofit finances get tighter and tighter, and as demands on the remaining funds accelerate due to everything from pensions to decaying infrastructure, the volumes of resources being allocated to incentives becomes more and more obvious. We all know that in most places we are well past cutting fat, and getting deep into muscle and bone.

And in a social media, networked, open data world where anyone with Excel on their laptop can analyze your funds and spending, the scrutiny focused on that funding is only going to grow.

Just the facts of the case, ma'am.

—

So what's the source of the systemic incentives illness? And how does anyone solve this?

> Incentives are easy. They are an intellectually and politically easy way to make it look like we are doing something good -- something that justifies our existence.

Here's the deep problem: incentives are easy. They are an intellectually and (until recently) politically easy way to make it look like we are doing something good -- something that justifies our existence. Company says they want incentives? You give them incentives, it makes them happy, you get a nice ribbon cutting and picture in the paper. Easy cheesy lemon squeezy.

Until people wise up to the fact that the golden ring they thought you had grabbed for them turns out to be painted plastic. Until they notice that the new retail center was followed by vacant storefronts in their neighborhood, or the cool tech company we all pinned our hopes on never lived up to its promises, or we got that great new office building that is supposed to lessen our tax burden, but we're still being asked to pass a huge school levy and the park district is turning off the lights.

Or they don't notice, but these things are happening, and then they cut your department to balance the budget.

Here's the deeper problem: we haven't been able to stop chasing those golden rings because we can't (or don't) figure out whether the ring is worth what it costs, or not.

Part of that has to do with the analytical problem that many writers, including Louise Story of the New York Times have identified -- the pervasive lack of postmortems, of doing the simple kind of look-backs that we know you have to do if you're going to learn from your failures -- or your successes.

But the bigger part of that deeper problem is that we have defined the cost of the ring too narrowly. One of the writers on the LinkedIn Economic Development 2.0 group said it clearly in describing his community's residents:

"The impression is that [first,] we aren't serving the public and second we aren't held accountable."

Does that make you cringe?

It made me cringe.

We like to assume that those new businesses and new jobs are having all sorts of benefits to the community. But what if they are not? What if they are cannibalizing another part of the local economy? Imposing costs on the local government that will cut its ability to support the community's quality of life? Putting the community at risk of agony down the road because that company that we bet the farm on didn't fit well, sold us snake oil or had no reason to stay when the incentives ran out? What if the cost of "progress" means destroying a heritage that the community will never be able to get back?

What if the costs are greater than the benefit? Did we look at both, or did we just see stars in our eyes at a bunch of pretty promises?

We want to think we can do our work in silos--that we are only responsible for our little bailiwick. It's easier that way. It's safer that way. But it's deadly, because what we do in one silo affects everything else. If we don't try to understand those interdependencies, or worse yet, ignore them in the name of "that's not my department," we dig ourselves and our communities ever deeper into the hole.

———

Here's the deepest problem of all: fixing this systemic illness, and making a difference for the communities we care about, requires professionals and elected officials and passionate community members to own their responsibility. We have no choice except to exercise the leadership that we alone can claim.

> Deals that look like wins on paper have the potential to hide cancers that will eat at the lives of our communities.

We have to stop accepting simplistic answers from our peers, department heads, or ourselves. We have to take leadership in teaching our elected leaders, bosses and communities what we know. We have to screw our courage to the sticking place and hold to our course.

We have to finally, finally give up on "shoot what flies and claim what falls." We have to admit what we know in our guts: deals that look like wins on paper have the potential to hide cancers that will eat at the lives of our communities.

Physician, heal thyself.

———

A small piece of encouragement for my professional economic development colleagues, who are likely to find this section the most challenging: in a broad sense, this challenge doesn't face economic developers alone. A couple of years ago, I took the urban and community planning profession to task for similar dangerous and damaging shortcomings -- particularly the tendency to avoid worrying about interdependencies and to stick in the silo your boss told you to stick in. It's strange to quote yourself, but, with a few word replacements, what I said to them fits here as well:

Stop allowing bad economic development. It's damaging the profession, and it's damaging the places that matter to us. Economic developers have had a tendency to avoid raising tough questions, to shy away from pushing for the right but difficult choices, to sidestep grappling honestly and critically with our decisions and alternatives.

That's mostly, I think, driven by a very understandable desire for job security. We have all been told somewhere along the line that some issues aren't in your job description, that you don't want to upset the politicians, the developers, the citizens, the client. Don't rock the boat, the voice whispers, and your job and your future are secure.

If there's anything the last few years have taught us, it's that job security, for both public and private sector employees, is a myth. Public sector employees get laid off or put on furloughs, or they get stuck in soul-deadening bureaucratic jobs processing paperwork and accept that deal with the devil for the promise of future financial security that is turning out to be a mirage. The private sector doesn't do much better: we deliver what the client wants, regardless of whether that's what the community needs or not, in the hopes of winning more work and maintaining that ridiculously high utilization rate and not having to spend nights and weekends writing more proposals on our "own time." And then we get laid off because of a "strategic realignment" or because the company wouldn't let us pivot to where the necessary work actually lies.

If we can't count on those promises, that security, and playing the incentive game is making it worse, then what is the price of our silence? Why not take reasonable, well-supported stands on issues that matter, when it matters? What have we really got to lose?

I say this because I have done all of these things. I did them because I was the consultant, it wasn't in the scope, it wasn't in the budget, they weren't "ready." I didn't want to rock the boat.

At the end of the day, what you're really left with is how you feel about the job you did. In some cases, I am proud of the work and how it helped move a community forward. In other cases, I am not sure whether my work did any good at all. As I evolve, I am determined to repeat those mistakes as few times as I can.

There's a piece of calligraphy in my office that sums up how I think we need to approach economic development in this generation -- not in terms of business clusters or recruitment strategies, but in terms of how we think about the job and how we think about communities and their futures. There are two quotes on it, the first being from Henry Thoreau:

Go confidently in the direction of your dreams. Live the life you have always imagined.

The second is from Will Rogers:

Even if you're going in the right direction, you'll get run over if you just sit there.

Let's not get run over anymore, ok?

How to Fix Incentives

We've been talking (or, well, not talking) about incentives in economic development in the U.S. They work, they don't work. They're necessary, they waste money. You need this control, that recapture method, no you don't, that's gonna backfire. So on and so on.

Perhaps it's time to take a big step back-- to revisit what an incentive was supposed to do in the first place. And perhaps it's time to confront where and how our practices are going awry, and re-formulate incentives programs-- not throw them away, not just control them better, but fix them, so that they do what our communities need, and so that they are worth the money we invest in them.

First, let's take the Wayback Machine to Econ Development 101:

The purpose of an economic incentive is to make something happen that market forces alone can't do. An incentive is supposed to exist to give the market a push in a direction that it can't/isn't going by itself at this moment. It's there to fill a gap.

Typically, says Econ Dev 101, the incentive is needed because the market can't see or isn't aware of an opportunity -- because it's a new opportunity, because the market is overlooking a location's potential due to negative assumptions about it, etc. The incentive is designed to kick-start the change, to get the market opportunity over that initial hump. That's why we started giving out incentives -- to overcome barriers to entry so that the potential of a labor pool or a technology or a place could be discovered by the market.

No one would say that the goal of an incentive is to replace the market, or contort the market, or fake up the market. But it's hard to miss that this is exactly what many incentives do.

So, if an incentive is supposed to do what Econ Dev 101 said, it follows that any incentive should have the following characteristics:

- **Time limited**--not just in terms of a specific deal having an expiration date, but time limited in availability.

  If the purpose of the incentive is to change the market, eventually the incentive should facilitate a change in the free market by demonstrating that a business type or a business location can actually work economically. If that case has been made -- if businesses can make a go of it -- then the incentive has done what it was designed to do, and it should not be offered anymore. Extending the incentive might be OK if that market opportunity still exists but hasn't fully taken off yet, such as might happen if an area experiences a natural disaster. But the incentive has to stop being available at some point. If it continues after the market no longer needs it, it's not levering the market -- it's distorting it.

  And a market that can't survive without the incentive may be too fragile, too risky to the surrounding community to be worth supporting.

- **Grow a market**. The incentive has to be targeted specifically to emerging or sleeper market opportunities -- like the "but for" test that many incentive programs at least give lip service to, but more so.

An incentive should be available, not just when Project X won't work without it, but when the larger market opportunity, with all of its potential, can't take off without it. The incentive shouldn't be about that specific business, although it may technically get applied to one business. An effective incentive will demonstrate potential to grow the opportunity -- to grow the market segment, the market ecosystem. To grow something that is bigger and more impactful than any one business.

The argument (the provable, demonstrable argument, as much as possible) has to be that incentivizing Project X will facilitate the growth of a whole sector, not just one firm.

Part of the reason why the focus has to shift from incentivizing one business to growing a market is that most of us aren't going to see many individual business opportunities that can single-handedly make a big impact on the local economy. We all know that businesses are getting smaller and smaller, and almost no one is seeing the four-digit employment investments anymore, no matter how much sugar they throw in the pot. If from nothing other than a pragmatic point of view, the purpose of an incentive has to be building an economic sector, not just one individual business, because any one individual business is going to be just a drop in the bucket of the job and investment growth our communities need.

A nice side benefit: an incentive that's focused on building a sector rather than a business can also spread out the risk. Instead of chewing our fingernails worrying that Business Y is going to renege on its incentive agreement, or move the day after the incentive runs out, or somehow otherwise break that supposed bond of trust and smear a lot of egg on our faces, an incentive strategy that focuses on building a sector should lessen the economic development initiative's dependence on any one business. If Business Y pulls something down the road, a strategy that has focused on using incentive money to build a sector, rather than just make Business Y happy, should have a decent chance at having created a larger system in which Business Y's employees, suppliers, etc. can find other beneficial options.

> So the question to ask isn't, "Do we need to do this incentive to get this business?"
>
> The real question is, "Are we building a base of human capital, expertise, relationships that can outlive any one business?"

So the question to ask isn't, "Do we need to do this incentive to get this business?" The real question is, "Are we building a base of human capital, expertise, relationships that can outlive any one business?"

Remember, businesses aren't just getting smaller, but there's lots of evidence that the life span of the average business is shrinking as well. So it makes less and less sense to bet the farm on one of them, even if that one looks really cool.

- **Grow Workforce capacity**. This point follows on to the need to feed the growth of a sector, not just a business. Whether we're talking about office, service, manufacturing, tech, whatever, we know more and more that the most valuable and most critical asset we can offer is the skills and capabilities of our workforce.

  If we need businesses to help us understand the sector's workforce needs, and people's capacities are at least partially built through their work experience -- and those businesses where they work become smaller and shorter-lived and generally more fluid everyday -- how much sense does it make to just hand businesses a piece of our precious funds and hope that something good will happen for its workers? Why not structure some conditions around building the capacity of their employees? Why not have an agreement about how they will support or participate in the training, networking, connection-building needed to grow their sector in your community?

  That's not going to ask much of them beyond basic good business practices (retain your employees because that's cheaper than hiring, build good relationships with your suppliers so you can get credit if you need it, etc.) You might as well give them a little extra push in that direction -- especially as businesses get smaller and owners and managers may not always fully realize how much they need to be part of the larger system. And since they're going to have to do at least some training, you're probably not adding significant cost.

- **Directly improve the community**. Here's one you know, but maybe don't want to say out loud:

  Citizens are sick of throwing their hard-earned tax money at businesses that they don't think give a damn about their community.
  Popular pressure is probably the biggest single threat to current incentives practices -- and as people get better at self-organizing, and as anyone with a mobile phone becomes their own broadcast network, that pressure is going to build. That's the nature of the social media, internet world. So why not give yourself some cover from the public watchdogs, and use incentives to prod businesses to be better community citizens?

  Plus, you've got precedent. Planning commissions routinely require developers who want a variance or special zoning to do a little extra -- more landscaping, higher quality facade materials, etc. If you, Madame Developer, don't want to do that, you can use the standard zoning without going through any extra process. But if you give us a little extra, you can use our expedited process or get special exemptions.

  Why not ask a potential incentive recipient, explicitly, how will you give back? How will you help build our community? How can you contribute as a corporate citizen?

After all, it's your taxpayers' money. They want more return on the investment. And sooner or later, that's what they're probably going to demand.

- **Manage our risk if the project doesn't work as we hope it will.** Clawbacks are fine in some cases, but if your goal is to facilitate meaningful change in the local economy, demanding the money back could backfire. Venture capitalists demand high returns, but they also expect that some of their investments will go belly-up. And in the tech world, which tends to be a leading indicator for a lot of other long-term growth sectors, the entrepreneur who has failed is often considered a better investment risk for next time, because presumably he/she has learned a few things that will make the next attempt better.

  Trying to grab the money back in a case like that could be shooting larger goals to grow a sector in the foot. Don't get me wrong, people absolutely have to be held responsible for their actions, and communities cannot just say "oh, well" and watch their money get piddled away on boondoggle projects and pipe dreams. But elaborate legal mechanisms to recapture as many red cents as possible may be less useful to communities than two other simple strategies: better evaluation of risks and benefits, and spreading the risks across more incentive recipients.

The poor overlooked stepchild in economic development is business retention, and its sidekick entrepreneurship. Let me rephrase: we give those two a lot of lip service anymore. A lot. But where does the money in the budget mostly go?

There's an old saw that says that where your treasure lies, there your heart lies. There's so, so much evidence that supporting local businesses and helping grow new businesses makes for a stronger economy long-term than does any recruitment. But if we know that, why does so much money go to incentives, and so little to doing meaningful things to help local businesses get better? What else can we do with our funds to improve their capacity and resilience? What training do they need? What connections? What information?

Part 3:

Your Secret Weapons

OK. So far, we've talked about

- How the world in which our local economies work has changed,
- The deep challenges of unintended consequences,
- Shifting our focus to enabling economic growth rather than trying to directly manipulate the machine,
- Leveraging assets instead of accepting the fate of a commodity,
- The potential impact of a small business focus, and
- The role of incentives.

All of that is well and good, but we live and work and try to make a difference in a political system, and political systems are made up of people, and people, all other things being equal, don't like change. So as you try to help your community manage this sea change, at some point you are going to get

Pushback
Resistance
Denial
Pointed Questions
A Fight

That's OK. It's a natural part of the process.

The legal and institutional reforms of the Progressive movement of the early 20th century, like city managers and housing standards, were to a great extent a response to the impacts of the Industrial Revolution, which started 70+ years before. And that was way, way quicker than the previous huge cultural shift, which was probably the Enlightenment.

So we're...what? 10 years into this one? 30? The concept of the laptop, which I'm writing this on, is 15, maybe 20 years old. The cell phone I keep fighting the temptation to check wasn't imaginable to me when my 22 year old son was born. Gar Alperovitz opens his book *What Then Must We Do?* by praising a new model of collaborative business ownership... one whose first attempt happened less than 40 years ago.[16] A blip in a culture's time frame.

This is gonna take a while. But it's going to happen, so you might as well help your community get on the leading edge of the wave, where all the good surfers want to hang. You can do that, even if some of your community's leadership hasn't seen the wave coming yet.

To help you stay in the curl (and lessen your odds of getting flattened by a rogue wave), this section focuses on your three secret weapons:

- Getting and using better information,
- Crowdsourcing wisdom,
- Bravery.

In both cases, since we're talking about what may be a relatively massive shift for your community, we'll start with some foundational tools and then start framing up the walls.

The first two won't completely prevent fights, challenges and resistance. But they'll help you make your case more clearly, give you some protections from

---

[16] Gar Alperovitz, *What then Must We Do? Straight Talk About the Next American Revolution.* Chelsea Green Publishing, White River, VT., 2013.

common misunderstandings, and most importantly, help you help your community understand what's going on.

Do keep one thing in mind: sometimes those who seem to be fighting you will have something valuable to add - something you'll want to hear and own up to and pull into the process. We always have the potential to screw it up, you know — and if we insist that we're infallible, we will set ourselves up for the same mistakes the "experts" of the previous generations did - while they dumped their unintended consequences on us. We, more than anyone, should know better.

And on top of all that, we had better be brave. That's the third secret weapon. More on that soon.

Secret Weapon #1:

Do Your Homework.

Homework?

That doesn't sound very weapon-y. My kid's paintball gun is more intimidating than that. Plus, it sounds... ugh.

I know. Sorry. If I could come up with something more exciting, I would. But the fact of the matter is, your ability to manage your community's sea change depends to a huge extent on how well you know your stuff - and how well you can avoid getting fooled by the trick questions.

Thankfully, you're not in differential calculus here. It's more like fourth grade math. It's more a matter of learning to do the work consistently than of hurting your brain cells with abstract concepts.

There's three key sections on your homework assignment:

- Making good decisions,
- Handling data, projections and estimates in a way that fits the Undercurrents, and
- Not letting consultants or other experts feed you a line of crap.

You need the first two so that you can do the third – kind of like you have to know how to do addition before you can do multiplication. So if you don't want to end up the hapless victim of some silver-tongued Fixer, let's make sure you do your homework.

The Logic of Failure: Making better plans

When our plans fail us, it's often because our blind spots, our limited assumptions and our overlooked mis-interpretations equipped us with a wrong or faulty strategy. We often set ourselves up for that failure because we didn't know and could not see all the things we were missing.

One of the books that has been most influential on my thinking over the past few years is a 20-year old volume with the catchy title *The Logic of Failure: Recognizing and Avoiding Error in Complex Situations* by Dietrich Dorner. The book details the results of a series of studies examining how people made decisions in complex and ambiguous environments.

> We often set ourselves up for that failure because we didn't know and could not see all the things we were missing.

Complex and ambiguous... sounds nothing like the communities we work with, right?

Add to that the fact that the participants were typically given economic development and public policy scenarios, and it starts to hit uneasily close to home.

In some respects, it's a depressing read. Participants in Dorner's studies make a lot more mistakes than correct decisions, and much of the time they fail, miserably. By studying the participants' choices and assumptions closely, and doing that a mind-numbing number of times, Dorner develops a pretty reliable differentiation between those who made consistently good decisions, and those who set themselves up for disaster again and again.

Dorner illustrates a large number of differences in how successful and unsuccessful participants approach and manage the tasks. Here is one that particularly stood out for me:

> Both the good and the bad participants proposed with the same frequency hypotheses on what effect higher taxes, say, or an advertising campaign to promote tourism in Greenvale [an imaginary city] would have. The good participants differed from the bad ones, however, in **how often they tested their hypotheses.** The bad participants failed to do this. For them, to propose a hypothesis was to understand reality; testing that hypothesis was unnecessary. Instead of generating hypotheses, they generated "truths."[17] [emphasis mine]

How often do we test our hypotheses? How often do we assume that a project will have a certain impact without taking a hard look at whether those assumptions are sound?

How often do we go back and re-examine the basic assumptions that we built our last plan on?

How often have we generated our own "truth," expended enormous resources on that truth, and then acted surprised when something hits us that we didn't see coming?

Admitting that we might not have the Truth takes bravery. Taking apart and examining the foundations of the structures we have built feels rightly dicey. But the termites work silently until the structure falls down.

Since we know that even our best ideas can create unintended consequences, one of the most important

---

[17] Dietrich Dorner, *The Logic of Failure: Recognizing and Avoiding Error in Complex Situations.* Basic Books, 1996. P. 26.

things we can do is test our hypotheses – regularly, not just during the plan development phase, but before, and after. We are perfectly capable of that. We just need to do it.

———

A follow-on piece of guidance from Dr. Michael Roberto of Bryant University, from the *Art of Critical Decision Making,* a Teaching Company lecture series. During the series, Dr. Roberto walks through two critical decision points of the John F. Kennedy presidential administration. During the first, the failed Bay of Pigs invasion in 1961, Kennedy made the decision to invade Cuba on the basis of advice from a small, relatively ad-hoc group of public policy advisors — a small group with so much "expertise" on the topic that they missed key information that fell outside their expectations... and set the invasion up for disaster.

When the Cuban Missile Crisis came along in 1962, Kennedy learned from that mistake, and he set up a completely different process for building his advisory team, establishing their objectives and enabling them to work through to a conclusion. More specifically, a conclusion that didn't end with a nuclear war.

Dr. Roberto provides this summary of a key lesson from the Kennedy experience:

> Many leaders fail because they think of decisions as events, not processes... We think of the decision maker sitting alone at a moment in time, pondering what choice to make. However, most decisions involve a series of events and interactions that unfold over time. Decisions involve processes that take place inside the minds of individuals, within groups, and across units of complex organizations.
>
> When confronted with a tough issue, we focus on the question, "what decision should I make?" **We**

should first ask, "how should I go about making this decision?" [emphasis mine]

In most cases, the source of what happens probably lies in how we decided to decide.

Which one can I eat?

We have a plethora of wisdom available to us in this era. We have developed tools to allow us to access unprecedented volumes of information and ideas, and you would think that this volume would allow us to find new solutions to our most complex public policy problems.

But obviously we haven't. Why?

My theory: we keep using simplistic methods for drawing meaning from that information, and that's stunting our ability to make strides forward. The next level of challenge that all of us in public policy face is to learn to use the information we have in a way that reflects the real complexity and interrelated character of the world around us.

One day, one of my Twitter contacts tweeted this:

While RI spent the last 5 years debating the extension of 1 airport runway 33 new airports have been built in China.

The simplicity of the statement bugged me – you don't have to be an international relations whiz to recognize that the comparison's not that simple.

In my usual Twitter fashion [that is, more to say than I can wedge into 140 characters, let along wedge in and be legible about it], I responded:

respectfl challge re China runways: @ wht cost? # Lost homes? Habitat, archeology etc destroyed? That's the impt diffce RI/China.

(Translation: Respectful challenge regarding China runways: at what cost? Number of lost homes? Habitat, archeology, etc. destroyed? That's the important difference between Rhode Island and China.)

My correspondent noted that *"cost/benefit analysis should inform not block all new initiatives."*

———

There's two possible ways to do this informing:

The first would be the conventional approach implied by cost/benefit analysis – economic issues, such as demand for air travel, have to be somehow "weighed" against intrinsically non-economic issues, such as environmental degradation. Both fine, and important, but different. The image we often use is one of "balancing." To see what I mean, picture the usual picture: two items on a mechanical scale:

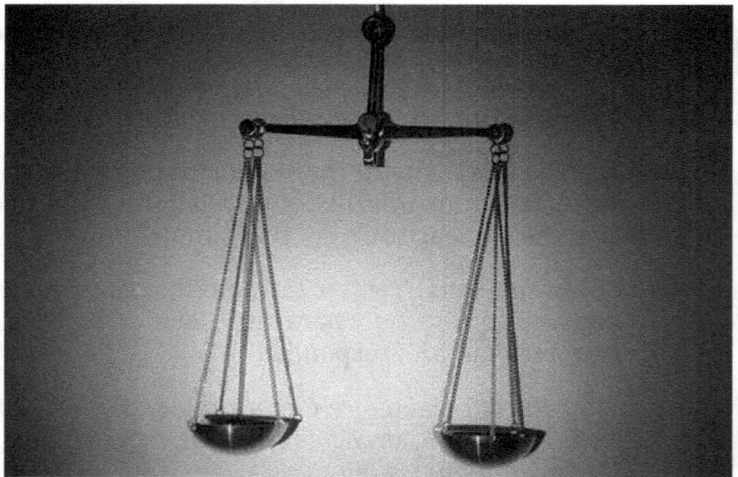

Photo by Sepehr Ehsani, used under Creative Commons 2.0 License

When we use cost-benefit analysis, what we are trying to do in essence is find a balance point between competing interests. The two items we are comparing are fundamentally different and fundamentally separate, things on opposite sides of that fulcrum. We put an apple on one side and a rock on the other, and we wait to see if what the balance does actually tells us something useful. But what does that comparison tell us?

(a rock is heavier than an apple)

What doesn't it tell us?

(which one can I eat?)

Which answer gives us something we can use?

No matter how fancy the graphs and tables, no matter how elaborate the calculations, the root method is the same: try to weigh the economic thing against an important but somehow non-economic thing, and hope that the numbers we get tell us something more useful than whether an apple is heavier than a rock.

This is part of why cost-benefit analyses of policy issues often fail to persuade people – they understand intuitively that a simple comparison probably misses important parts of the story.

———

Our fundamental approach to public policy analysis needs to be re-evaluated – not because you *can't* make comparisons, but because the assumption that non-economic things, such as environments or social opportunity, are *in themselves not the same as economic things*, is a fundamentally false assumption. What we so easily forget, and what we increasingly must not forget, is that these things are not discrete lumps sitting on separate trays: the issues that we are inclined to call non-economic are central to the function of a vibrant economy.

We talked in a previous chapter about externalities. Externalities are impacts of economic choices that fall outside of the transaction that the economist wants to look at. If I buy 20 head of cattle and put them on my third of an acre suburban lot, that decision might make sense for me economically (I like milk), but it creates externalities for my neighbors (her damn cows stink and moo and ate my flowers, and now my property value is lower because no one wants to buy my house and live next to all that).

If we see beyond the simplistic example discrete things on a balance, and we start thinking instead about the potential flows of externalities, the impacts and the unintended consequences of the choices we make, then we can begin to make real sense about whether one choice or another is the most wise. If we focus on the connections and the impacts, we end up with more and better information than simply whether an apple is lighter or heavier than something else.

If we think about supposedly non-economic impacts in terms of their pervasive, direct and indirect potential economic impacts, the value of those non-economic things changes substantially. There are direct and indirect impacts of the different methods that Rhode Island and China have taken to address their air travel needs, and the impacts of those choices on the long-term health of their economic system. That's the important question: what's the entire impact on the vitality of the economy, not just who builds more runways.

Suddenly we are evaluating two elements of the same system – two species of apples, not an apple and a rock.

And with that manner of observation, we can finally use the information we have to make wise decisions.

What about the Opportunity Costs?

In addition to externalities, the other thing that we often don't address clearly enough when we make a decision are the opportunity costs. An opportunity cost is the value of the choice I decided *not* to pursue - the value of the thing I could have had if I had made a choice different from the one I did.

When I went back to graduate school at the age of 30, my opportunity cost was the value of the salary I could have been earning if I hadn't been spending all my time on school. For me, the value resulting from that degree's potential to move me into a more lucrative career exceeded the value of the income I might have earned otherwise. But if the degree had cost me $1 million, or I'd been a successful investment banker before, then the opportunity cost would have been too high, and I would have made a different choice.

Far too many of the organizations trying to improve our communities explicitly identify or analyze opportunity costs. Part of the problem we have with changing how we do economic development, and particularly how we deal with the incentives question, is that we don't systematically and rationally evaluate what else we could be doing with those funds. We don't figure out what our opportunity costs are — what other impact we could get from that pot of money, and how the benefits and likelihood of payoff compare.

An economic development opportunity cost evaluation system would rotate around three pretty basic questions:

1. If we didn't do X, what are the most likely other things we could do with this funding/ staff time/ surplus building/ whatever?
2. What benefits would we get from those other options?
3. What's the value of what we would give up by choosing to do Project X instead of one of them?
4. Given that, is Project X the right choice?

It's not complicated, it just requires some honest thought. And it's just a matter of time before someone else does that math and forces us to confront opportunity costs more explicitly. So we might as well start doing it.

The Fallacy of The Number[18]

An article published in the *Journal of the American Planning Association* in 2002 claimed that economic evaluations for large projects – the kinds of evaluations often done when public dollars are sought to support a project - are intentionally underestimated.[19] The author claimed in another publication, years later, that those evaluations deliberately lied about the projected economic impact of projects, and that professionals in the planning and development world were covering that up.[20]

The economic evaluations we often use to support large projects often have problems, lots of problems. But the author focused on the wrong piece of the equation. Of course, there will always be an occasional "bad apple" who has intentionally misled people, or a major miscommunication that leaves someone feeling cheated.

---

[18] Adapted from Peter Mallow, "Economic Impact Studies: The Number is not your friend."
http://wiseeconomy.com/economic-impact-the-number-is-not-your-friend/

[19] Bent Flyvbjerg, Mette Skamris Holm, and Søren Buhl. "Underestimating Costs in Public Works Projects Error or Lie?" *APA Journal* Vol. 68, No. 3 (Summer 2002) 279-295.

[20] "Mean streets: Expert on lying accuses planning association of ethical lapses."
http://retractionwatch.wordpress.com/2013/02/19/mean-streets-expert-on-lying-accuses-planning-association-of-ethical-lapses/

But there's a far more common problem that I see when it comes to understanding and using economic evaluations:

Ignorance.

With all the demands on our time, some ignorance is to be expected. Almost by definition, we all have to be generalists in most things we encounter. And because of that, we often feel that we need an expert to tell us what economic impact a new project will generate, or how the cost and benefits will stack up, or how many TIF dollars it's going to put in the fund.

In some cases, we simply rely on the project applicant's own economic evaluations because we don't have the resources to hire our own consultant or buy the software package that promises to spit out that number for you. In other cases, we get our own consultant or software, but the fundamental problem remains the same.

Here's the problem: it's easy, very easy, to rely on an expert or software package that promised to give you a "certain" answer. That certain answer? It's The Number, the one specific number that everyone clings to promote the project.

You have most likely encountered The Number. The Number tells you how many new jobs, how much investment, how much tax revenue, etc. is going to come as a result of the investment.

People love The Number. Decision makers love having a clear answer to point to, and the media loves having simple factoid that it can easily report.

Because of that, The Number becomes its own living creature, and the project skeptics and detractors can only wait for the inevitable.

The inevitable?

The inevitable, unexplained, and unexplored uncertainty that is buried in the assumptions and methods behind The Number.

At some point in the future, a seemingly innocuous assumption will change and the actual impact of the project will change dramatically. When that happens, the project skeptics and detractors will pounce.

And guess who gets caught in the crossfire.

—

So what do we do? Too often, we think that our only choice is to accept The Number and deal with the inevitable down the road. After all, we will argue, we don't have the time or the technical wizardry to pick apart the methods and the assumptions embedded in The Number.

And many of you would probably add: the money won't allow it, either.

That's all true. But let me propose an alternative.

If somebody, anybody, tries to sell you on The Number, the only thing you can be certain of is that The Number will be wrong.

Think about a stock investment for a minute. You have no idea what the value will be in five years...or one year. You hope it will be higher than today. But would a trustworthy financial advisor assure you that the $10,000 you invest in a stock today will be worth $15,552.35 in one year? Or $32,535.97 in five years?

Of course not. They will give you a range of the most likely future values under different growth or loss scenarios.

Instead of accepting The Number, demand to know the plausible range of jobs, tax dollars, economic impact, etc., given what we know. Or ask for some different scenarios: what happens to The Number if the building doesn't fill up as fast as they project, or the average payroll turns out to be less, or the cost of steel spikes in the middle of construction. What then?

You can do that. And you and your community will be better off for it. After all, you're not evil. And you're not even really ignorant. You just need to know what to demand, and demand it.

Impact Analysis: Two Common Mistakes[21]

The Number generated by an economic impact analysis gives us a potentially powerful estimate of the jobs and dollars a new project or program will bring to your community. The Number also makes it easy to build support when existing local institutions ask for public money.

And that's a problem, because often The Number stretches the truth: it pretends jobs or dollars are being added to the economy when they actually aren't.

Let's imagine a place that develops an economic impact statement to help it ask for money. Maybe it needs a tax levy renewed, maybe it's trying to get approval for a loan guarantee or a subsidy. Let's give it a catchy name – let's call it the Favored Community Institution. For our purposes, the Favored Community Institution could be pretty much anything: an arts organization, a zoo, a major employer, an education institution, a professional sports team, a major tourist attraction.

When an economic impact analysis is prepared for a Favored Community Institution, we need to look hard for a couple of very important considerations so that we know how much to trust The Number that comes out of it.

———

---

[21] Adapted from Peter Mallow, "Guess what? The Number might be pretending! Two common mistakes in economic impact analysis." http://wiseeconomy.com/guess-what-the-number-might-be-pretending-two-common-mistakes-in-economic-impact-analysis/

First, economic impact analyses are amoral. That's a-moral (not immoral).

Because of its catchy name, you know that the Favored Community Institution holds a cherished spot in the history of the community, and most people have positive attachments to that institution. When they give us The Number, it reinforces the strength of the attachment – "Not only is it fun to visit, but look, it puts money into our economy, too!"

Keep in mind, however, that an economic impact analysis does not tell us if the Favored Community Institution is better than any other institution in the community. As a decision-maker, an economic impact analysis cannot answer the question that you really have to answer:

Is this an appropriately beneficial use of precious public money?

An example may help explain this distinction.

Let's imagine that the Favored Community Institution is not a happy place like a zoo or a tourist destination. Instead, the Favored Community Institution is a grenade factory. It employs a few hundred people who build and ship grenades all over the world. The Favored Community Grenade Factory has been in town as long as anyone remembers, and its leadership serves the community on various boards and elected offices.

The Favored Community Grenade Factory wants to retool due to high demand for their grenades. The expansion will create new jobs and bring new dollars to the community from the increased production. They even have an economic impact analysis showing a large

Number of new dollars that will be brought into the community. But they can't do it without a public subsidy for new roads and rail connections.

Here's the public policy question: Is this is an appropriately beneficial use of limited public money, even though its existence is predicated on people dying?

What about the brand-new, farmer's market on the other side of town? An infusion of public dollars will allow them to employ more people, expand their parking, buy more from local farmers, and make people healthier.

Which one deserves the money?

We want to think that all economic impacts are good economic impacts, but we know in real life that not everything is good for us (like grenades versus farmer's markets). Economic impact analysis doesn't help us make value judgments or compare the non-monetary impacts of different institutions.

—

Second, a technical issue, but a very critical one: if a Favored Community Institution is already part of the community, then *only new* dollars or jobs should be included in the economic impact analysis. But that often doesn't happen.

The standard economic impact analysis method is based on the assumption that the proposed project will bring new money into the community. The new money creates a "shock" that reverberates within the community. The shock created by the new money is the multiplier effect – the promise that the new money will generate additional jobs and money circulation beyond the initial investment. As a result, what that multiplier effect gives you is the amount of new (revenue, jobs, etc.) that will result from that investment.

But our Favored Community Institution is generating at least some of those impacts today, before the proposed investment. Many economic impact analyses don't separate those out. They calculate the impact based on the total value of what's there today *and* what's proposed. That basic overlooked assumption violates the fundamentals of economic impact analysis.

When existing jobs and spending are included in the analysis, The Number will be grossly overstated because the community has already absorbed the existing jobs and spending. We are, in essence, double-counting.

Think back to our Favored Community Institution for a moment (the happy one, not the grenade factory). Let's say that it currently employs 100 people. It is looking to expand, and it's requesting $5 million in publicly-funded improvements. This expansion will generate 50 new jobs. The Number that they gave you in their economic impact analysis said that over 200 service and support jobs would be generated by the proposed expansion.

They've made a gross overstatement of The Number. If they were introducing 250 new jobs into the community, then they might generate 200 to 300 new service and support jobs. But according to any kind of reasonable estimate, 50 new jobs might support 75 to 100 service and support jobs.

So, does the Favored Community Institution deserve those additional public funds? Well, it's complicated … and the answer has to include factors outside of the economic impact analysis.

But don't be misguided by The Number – at the end of the day, The Number only says what it says, and is only as good as the thought that went into it.

Consultant as Wizard: Bullshit

It's very hard to type and pace around fuming at the same time.

Last year I left a session at a national conference because I was too mad to be civil anymore. I wrote at the time:

"I am beyond tired of consultants feeding communities bullshit in the guise of wisdom. No wonder they don't trust us."

The session I left was on using economic impact studies to determine whether financial incentives are appropriate in economic development. I had just taught a class on unraveling economic impact studies with Pete Mallow, so that part was somewhat of interest, and I was teaching a training on use of incentives next month, so that part was the reason I went.

I had to leave halfway through before my budding anger and bad behavior got me in trouble.

The speaker, whom I don't know, presented that slick all-knowing persona *de rigeur* (along with a head of gray hair). His message?

"Look how nice and straightforward and objective all of your incentives negotiations will be if you base them on the crystal clarity that an economic impact study (especially if done by us or using our software) gives you.

"You want to know what an economic impact study includes? Well, first you take your direct costs, you plug them into the magic calculator, hocus pocus and...

"Voila! Here's your number. Now you know what your incentives should be. Doesn't that make you feel good?

"Want to project it out 10 years into the future? No problem. How easy we've made it for you!

"How did we get that number, you ask? Here's the name of our magic multiplier source...that's all you need to know, you know. Don't worry about it. Trust us... We're the experts."

Bullshit.

This is *not* the answer to the incentives conundrum, or the larger question of figuring out what we should do. All this does is make it worse.

There is no way that an economic analysis is worth the memory it takes up in your inbox unless you understand exactly how that magic number was calculated and why the multipliers used were used.

If the multipliers are straight out of some standard source, and your community is not identical in time and space to the geography used in that source, the analysis will not fit.

Worse, there is no way in hell that a 10-year projection that lands on one number can be right. It's statistically impossible. Any honest person who passed college statistics can tell you that.

Common sense when you think about it. And yet, people keep buying it.

A roomful of people sat and listened and took notes and bought it.

Bullshit.

———

Is it any wonder why consultants who work with local governments have such a bad reputation? In a complex, unpredictable, variable world, how can we offer simple, easy, prepackaged solutions... and sleep at night? How can we stay behind the curtain of the wizard's facade in Oz without constant fear of being uncovered?

How much of the physical, fiscal, economic mess that our communities face can be laid at the feet of know-it-all consultants who offered easy, unrealistic answers... and never addressed the alternatives, the externalities, the unintended consequences?

How many times can we who are consultants leave a mess in our wake, relying on the fact that we can find another sucker down the road who won't know about how badly we got this one wrong?

What's it going to take before communities learn to call us on it?

What's it going to take before we come to terms with our own lack of omniscience?

When are we finally going to shift from arrogant know-it-all to what we should really be:

Advisors and facilitators. Listeners. Resources. Sources of perspective. Guides. Teachers.

Until then, what good do we do?

———

I try to do the right thing, but I've described before how sometimes I've been guilty of telling a community what they want to hear instead of what they need to hear. I try not to do that anymore.

But it takes two to polka. You who work for and care about communities have a role to play here, too. And that role is:

- To not accept the bullshit.

- To not assume that a grey haired dude in a suit automatically knows how to lead you to the promised land.

- To ask questions. Ask a lot of questions. Ask the stupid questions. Ask more questions if you don't fully understand the answer.

Under no circumstances accept anything that even hints at "we're the experts, trust us." We should have learned by now that that dog don't hunt.

If your consultant gives you a magic number out of a black box, chase him out of town. If your consultant makes it sound too easy, push for the details, probe for the grey areas.

And if your consultants even begin to condescend to you, fire their ass. Period. They are not doing you any good.

And that's true if I show up as your consultant, too.

What a consultant is good for

Um, Della. You keep beating up on consultants. You've been a consultant for close to 25 years. You still make money consulting.

You like to eat, don't you?

Hm.

I'm starting to understand why I might not be the biggest money maker among consultants.

Traditional consulting relies on the expectation of the know-it-all expert. The glossy genius in the sweeping cape who tells you exactly what your town needs and withers you with his glare if you dare to question him.

The Guy With The Answers. The Oracle. The Fixer. The Big Name.

But here's the problem: we all know how many times the people we (or our predecessors) thought were Experts in the past turned out to be... wrong. Sometimes badly wrong. Sometimes painfully, decades-long wrong. The kind of wrong that we spend generations trying to dig out of, and that the people we did them to try to heal from.

And yet we buy the next set of promises. The next expert. The next promised easy answer, wrapped in a flowing aristocratic cape.

Naveen Jain laid the basic problem out in a previous chapter. It's essentially a problem of methodology: traditional experts rely on historical trends, on what worked in the past, on their own, often unexamined assumptions.

That's how we define an "expert," after all. How many years have you been doing this? How many projects have you done that were *just like ours?*

The problem is this: if much of what has been done in our consultants' lifetimes hasn't worked, if much of it didn't really do what we hoped for, and if the challenges we're facing are wicked and complex and new and interrelated, then what makes us think that a past book of experience alone counts very much?

Part of what gets me so mad is that neither the consultants nor the people who hire consultants admit or face up to these limitations. Both sides keep pretending-one that it has all the answers, the other that there are simple answers to be had.

In their guts both sides have to know that neither charade is true.

Or maybe they don't know that. Maybe they know but don't want to know. Do they?

Now I'm not sure what to get madder about.

—

Years ago, I managed comprehensive planning projects for a consulting firm. When you start one of those, you get to review pretty much every plan that town has ever done. And sometimes what you find yourself reviewing is a case history in delusion.

One community, struggling to find a bright future for a run-down suburban strip, spent a huge sum on a beautiful drawing of lovely new buildings lining the streets. They also bought a rudimentary market analysis that indicated nothing about whether the lovely buildings could ever be funded through the private investment that the drawing promised. And then the community threw significant sums of money and effort into finding the people who would build that grand vision.

Twenty years later, the corridor hasn't changed, except for continuing to fall apart. I drove down it last week.

If you're a former client of mine, and you think I'm talking about your town, it's probably not. I can tell that same story about 15 different communities.

—

So, Consultant as Wizard doesn't work. Should you ditch them entirely, rely just on yourselves, figure out all out the best you can? Are the non-experts enough?

No. Chances are you definitely need outside help. You just need a different type of help than many consultants have been giving.

In this era, I think an intellectually truthful, community-benefitting consultant has to hang up the cape, drop the all-knowing charade, and take on jobs like these:

1. **Guide through the Unknown.** Adventurers like Robert Peary, who trekked to places people had never been, took people with them who had experience in that *type of environment*, although not in *that exact situation.* Chances are that you, Ms. Consultant, don't know the path any better than they do, but you've at least moved through an environment somewhat like this before.

   So we don't charge into the underbrush, pretending that you know where all the rocks and rattlesnakes lie, but we walk with them and help them figure out how to best navigate.

2. **Framework builder.** When we can't plug and play easy solutions, when we have to find our way through unknown territory, building mental frameworks gives us a way to evaluate options, think through the potential impacts of our choices and plan ahead for risks. A consultant' s experience can help build intelligent and flexible frameworks. But a framework is not a blueprint, and it's not a Magic Solution. It recognizes that it might be wrong and that it might have to shift and evolve over time. It's an exercise in managing uncertainty with the best intelligence we can bring to the table. And since the framework is designed to enable shifting and evolving, it might actually continue to fit more than three weeks after the consultant's last bill gets paid.

3. **Tough question-asker.** People who lead communities often fail to ask hard questions - you know, the

unpleasant ones where we suspect the answers are not what we want to hear, or where the answers aren't clear at all. In far, far too many cases, communities get into deep trouble because no one asked the hard questions - either because no one knew what to ask, or because no one summoned the bravery to ask it.

By rights, and as a matter of integrity, the consultant should be the one to ask the hard questions when no one else can or will do it. After all, the consultant is the one who gets to go home to Somewhere Else when the meeting is over. More importantly, though, the consultant can draw on that expertise, that guiding capability, to call out and articulate the questions that no one from the community can or wants to own.

But too many consultants never ask the tough questions -- because they don't want to piss off the client, they don't want to knock themselves out of consideration for the next project.

Mostly because, at the end of the day, consultants really, deeply want you to like them.

So we let the client believe what they want to believe, and avoid the problems they don't want to face. After all, the consultant is the one who gets to go home to Somewhere Else when the meeting is over. And there's always another one, some town somewhere else where we can proclaim that this project was Fantastic!! somewhere around the bend.

4. **Decision pusher**. Communities often don't ask tough questions, and lots of them try to avoid making decisions. That's where the laundry list plan failure that I've talked about before comes from, as well as a lot of other problems ranging from underfunded pensions to crumbling water lines. Decisions are hard, you know... they mean saying yes to some things and

no to others. And we won't even talk about setting priorities. Ow.

The consultant's job has to include guiding, structuring, pushing and cajoling a community to make a decision. It just has to. It has to be done, and I don't know an honest consultant who hasn't been around the block enough times to know that in their guts. If the community doesn't make important decisions, if we haven't done everything in your power to get them to do it, I don't think we've earned our fee. If they flat out refuse, so be it. But too often we who have the experience and framework to make out the rocks in the water ahead are too timid to tell the captains that they need to change course.

Consultants don't want to push people to make decisions, either, for all of the same reasons as above. But unless they do, the effort is probably wasted.

Communities definitely need consultants. The difference I see is this:

The consultant that communities need is a *collaborator*, a fellow-seeker who brings a new set of expertise, a new collection of tools, to the work of improving your community.

We who do consulting work for communities have to deeply rethink what we provide as consultants, and we who work for communities have to deeply rethink what we demand from our consultants. Settling for a pretty picture of an imagined future, or a kum-ba-yah list of all the happy things everyone in town said they wanted, is worse than a waste of money.

It's setting up the community for a future crushing of hope, a long-term trend of growing cynicism and tuning out. And it's setting up the community for painful opportunity costs - wasted resources chasing unachievable pipe dreams.

Letting a community persist in mistaken optimism or pessimism or inertia is not morally, ethically or fiscally acceptable, for consultants or for community professionals. We simply don't have that much slack in the system anymore. Consultants should - and must - help a community fill the gaps in its capacity to make wise choices and tough decisions possible.

Secret Weapon 2:

Crowdsource Wisdom

Note: in 2015, I wrote a book called <u>Crowdsourcing Wisdom.</u> And in 2018, I wrote one called <u>Everybody Innovates Here</u>. Those books go into more detail about a couple of different approaches to this topic.

Hi. My name is Della, and apparently I look like this:

From <u>Barrygott.com</u>. I didn't ask permission because he's my brother. So check out his books for me, OK?

When I started my business a couple of years ago, I settled on the Wise Economy name because I tend to see everything I do through the filter of whether or not it fosters long term economic health. The original business plan included a cumbersome five service lines, one of which was traditional public engagement, which I'd done for years as a planner.

I've learned in the process that there's not much overlap between the public engagement people and the economic development types. And that those are often seen as completely unrelated professions. Even after spending a lot of years in local government consulting, that surprised me.

Here's the thing: in my head, at least, economic revitalization and public engagement aren't two unrelated things. They are critically intertwined, and we screw both of them up when we try to do one and don't deal with the other.

We depend on our economies. We live in a world where economic decision making either sets a community up for success or drives it deeper into a hole. And we live in a world where the economy that we all depend on doesn't look much like it did not long ago. If we want healthy, desirable communities that will stay that way for a long time, we have to deal with its economic conditions.

And yet, when we deal with economic development, we tend to treat that as an insider game. We claim confidentiality or that "it's too complicated," and we confine our planning and strategy to a star chamber of ED types, elected officials and a few Blue Ribbon Committee business leaders.

Then, when we propose The Big Project, the community fights it, raising ill-informed (or maybe just uncomfortable) questions about real economic impacts, or community side-effects. They don't make it easy, and sometimes their scrutiny kills our pet project.

Rubes. Don't they know anything?

Similarly, when communities do "public engagement," we tend to ask people questions in a way that's divorced from economics, as though dealing with the dollars and cents that determine whether a choice can become reality or not would somehow sully the truthfulness of the public input. Long range planning projects are the worst for this - "what do you want to see here?"

Not surprisingly, we get dreams, we get idealistic visions. We get Santa Claus letters.

Then, when the plan comes out, those residents turn out torqued that the economically impossible answer they gave didn't make it into the plan. Or we put the fantasy in with full realization that there's nothing in there to help make it happen. In either case, the damage is done:

"They didn't listen to us." "They didn't really want our feedback." "Public meetings are a waste of time."

We need to do a lot of things better in economic development planning, but our most critical need may be to help people clearly understand and evaluate their community's economic options and the potential consequences of those choices. And we need to do a whole lot better at public engagement, but perhaps the most important is to use the process to help people apply their insight within realistic economic boundaries.

Most important, whichever we're doing, we have to admit that we don't have all the answers, and that we need to crowdsource as much wisdom as we can get. That doesn't mean the public has some perfect set of answers, but it does mean that we need the community's perspective and experience, just like they need our expertise.

We need both wise community engagement and wise economic decision making. They're part of the same mission. And we have to get them working together.

Go find some Non-Experts. You probably need them

We have an increasing number of voices that are challenging the assumption that past experience correlates to ability to solve current problems- especially those that are fundamentally different from what has happened before. In that setting, relying on experience can hobble, rather than help.

One person who has written about this is _Naveen Jain_. Jain can claim pretty decent cred on this topic -- he has founded multiple tech firms, he's a trustee of the X Prize Foundation.... when it comes to innovative problem-solving for complex issues, this guy knows his stuff.

Here's what he wrote in Forbes -- I'm excerpting heavily, but do go read the whole column later:

> ...[P]eople who will come up with creative solutions to solve the world's biggest problems...will NOT be experts in their fields. The real disruptors will be those individuals who are not steeped in one industry of choice, with those coveted 10,000 hours of experience, but instead, individuals who approach challenges with a clean lens, bringing together diverse experiences, knowledge and opportunities....

> Experts, far too often, engage in a kind of myopic thinking. Those who are down in the weeds are likely to miss the big picture. To my mind, an expert is in danger of becoming a robot, toiling ceaselessly toward a goal but not always seeing how to connect the dots.

> The human brain, or more specifically the neo-cortex, is designed to recognize patterns and draw conclusions from them. Experts are able to identify such patterns related to a specific problem relevant to their area of knowledge. But because non-experts lack that base of

knowledge, they are forced to rely more on their brain's ability for abstraction, rather than specificity. This abstraction -- the ability to take away or remove characteristics from something in order to reduce it to a set of essential characteristics -- is what presents an opportunity for creative solutions.

I also believe that the value of expertise is diminished in a world dominated by two trends: the accelerating pace of innovation and the ubiquity of information....The digital revolution has also meant a revolution in access to information. This puts more power and knowledge into the hands of non-experts... Granted, they alone don't make us experts -- but they give us access to information in abundance, giving us a greater base from which to "think big."[22]

Two implications for those of us who work with communities:

1. Once we realize that our communities are in a moment where they desperately need what the business world calls "discontinuous innovation," then the **questions that we have to ask** our consultants, our boards, our Blue Ribbon Panels, and ourselves undergo a sea change. A large number of years of experience might be a liability, rather than an asset, if it means we will stick with the tried-and-true that may not work anymore, or may not work for your community. Can we shift

---

[22] Naveen Jain, "Rethinking the Concept of "Outliers": Why Non-Experts are Better at Disruptive Innovation." *Forbes,* July 12, 2012. http://www.forbes.com/sites/singularity/2012/07/12/rethinking-the-concept-of-outliers-why-non-experts-are-better-at-disruptive-innovation/

away from the methods we've used before if they don't fit now? Intellectual flexibility, the ability to tap that power of abstraction and connect those dots, rather than start doing the Robot, may be the most important skill we can assemble at our table.

2. The good news is that we have an **enormous supply of non-experts** who can "approach challenges with a clean lens, bringing together diverse experiences, knowledge and opportunities." We call them the Public. They know stuff. They've done stuff. They have the power of abstraction that those of us in the weeds struggle to grasp. We have to set them up to succeed, but if we do, they might present our best opportunity for the discontinuous innovation that we need. After all, us experts haven't solved the problems yet.

Maybe it's time to bring in the real experts.

The three main barriers to meaningful public engagement

One of the biggest, often overlooked challenges we are facing today is that our traditional debate model of public involvement isn't working, and it's probably outlived its usefulness. There's at least three reasons for that.

First, **the traditional stand-up-and-make a speech approach evolved in an epoch when public participation was limited to a much more narrow portion of the total population than we know we need to involve today.** Nineteenth – century politics (back to the ancient Greeks, actually) was limited to reasonably educated white men. So even when there were differences of opinion on local issues, everyone in the room was coming from, in very broad terms, the same perspective. Today, we have a lot more voices, a wider range of voices, and not everyone knows how to express themselves adequately within that oratory model. So we get silence from a large part of the population, and often less than ennobling wisdom from the small number who stand up to speak.

The second reason is that **the issues we have to grapple with have become much, much more complicated because of the interdependencies and inter**relationships that we live within in a modern community. You can't deal with too much complexity, address too many nuances and acknowledge that there may not be a perfect solution when you are at a podium for three minutes and the situation has been cast as a for-or-against debate.

The third issue is that the ways in which we gain understanding and grapple with decisions are changing. K-12 educational methods (how teachers are being taught to teach) have largely discarded the lecture as a useful means of building knowledge.

Instead, teachers are increasingly shifting to methods that engage the students directly in dealing with the information, making sense out of it for themselves – which means that they develop better and more meaningful solutions to the problems they are presented. Frankly, that should have happened a long time ago. Cognitive psychiatrists have known for generations that only a very, very small part of the population learns best by listening to someone talk. And the more we become used to living in a world rich with information of all types, the more we need to be able to do more than parrot back what we hear.

What does educational methodology have to do with public participation? Everything.

What we desperately need is for our citizens to do much more than spout ill-informed NIMBYisms or buy into knee-jerk, simplistic cause-effect assumptions. We need to

- Draw on the unique knowledge, perspective and expertise of everyone we can get,

- Get them reasonably up-to-speed on the issues, and

- Engage them – get their hands deeply into – the search for solutions... solutions that are realistic and address the complexities and ambiguities of real community life.

Major companies put massive amounts of effort into broadening their employee base to include the widest range of people possible and then creating team environments to work on solving complex challenges. If they're finding it necessary to use diverse team problem-solving to deal with stuff like getting shampoo into a bottle, how much more do we desperately need real, deep involvement to deal with the massive complexities that make up a community?

—

It's not simply a matter of throwing a bunch of people in a room with a problem and hoping that they'll figure something out. That'd be foolish.

Instead, we who work with communities have to borrow a page from good teachers and good business team managers: we have to

- Carefully create a **structure** that moves people through the information they need efficiently,

- **Channel** their efforts into the right direction,

- Make it **safe** for everyone to participate (including your sweet grandmother who never speaks in public), and

- Lead them to the **creation of something that has value** to the community and makes the time and effort they spent worthwhile.

The tools to do this are out there. We just have to learn them and use them.

Why community involvement requires a structured approach, even when we're seeking new ideas

When communities and nonprofits do public engagement, we often fuss about how we keep getting "the Usual Suspects." But we often do little more than fuss. I can think of two different broad categories of "not the usual suspects," and both of them will need a different strategy if we truly want them to participate.

First, the public participation methods we traditionally use tend to exclude the less educated, immigrants, those who do not speak our language well. Again, this isn't some do-gooder thing —we need to include them because these people have a particular knowledge of the community that we will never be able to access if they don't share that with us. If we remain blind to the issues they know about, we'll miss the opportunities to address them, which is likely to have a direct impact on our community's tax base growth and the demand for community services.

I've done public involvement sessions co-led with a trusted community translator or liaison to draw out participation from immigrant communities. If there is any expectation of persons who are illiterate or disabled, I make sure that it's known in the information that goes out before the event that people will be available to help those who have trouble reading or writing. I'll often also station a person at a table to write down any comments or ideas that anyone has. That helps not only people who cannot write or elderly people who have trouble seeing, but it also helps people who can write but would rather just proclaim their ideas. That way we get their thoughts down, and they feel like they've said their piece, but we haven't let them dominate the entire community's discussion.

A second type of resident that is typically underrepresented is younger adults. There's at least two barriers to their involvement, and both of them derive from our continuing to use these outdated public involvement models.

First, you're dealing with a population that has a lot of demands on their time -- jobs, kids' activities, social events, etc. If I am in that boat (and I was), asking me to sit in an auditorium and listen to someone drone about what may or may not be a key issue to them...that's a luxury many can't afford, and it's a very unclear return on investment for giving up a very valuable commodity: my time.

I am probably more aware of the impacts that local government decisions have on the rest of life than most people in my age group, so you would think I would be at my community's council and planning commission meetings all the time. But given the choice to spend two hours of my evening sitting in a meeting where I might or might not be able to give meaningful participation, while at the same time I have kids who need to get to practice, a house that needs cleaning, flower beds that need weeding and a report to write that I should have done last week... it's extremely hard for me to make that equation work in favor of going to the meeting.

Needless to say, if I have anything better to do with my time than go to that public hearing and listen to the crabby people ramble, I'll be doing that instead of the public hearing.

The second barrier is the changes I alluded before to how younger people tend to think and interact with information. For people - let's say generally 45 and younger - the combination of inefficiency, lack of ability to actively engage in the process and, let's face it, the often confrontational and overly simplistic rhetoric you hear in the typical public meeting is completely off-putting.

I think this generation is particularly aware of the ineffectiveness of this approach because they haven't come up that way - they have come of age and entered the workforce in collaborative problem-solving teams. And they have more clear memories of how often they fell asleep during college lectures.

Engaging this population takes an entirely different approach. First, we need to make it more convenient to accommodate the busy. This is where online methods become so important - not just because they are cool and whiz-bang, but because they do not require me to be in a certain place at 7 PM. I can participate at midnight after the baby has gone back to sleep, or at 6 AM while eating breakfast, or wherever. If I expect to be able to buy a pair of shoes online from my phone at 2 AM, certainly I am going to expect that I can interact with my local government at any time of day or night, when I have the time.

Second, that interaction has to be more meaningful than just "I like it" or "I hate it." This population expects to be able to be part of the conversation, and they increasingly expect a rich, interesting and well - managed experience. Again, all of this is not nearly as hard as it might sound - it all depends on finding and using the right existing tools.

Who's the Unrealistic One Here?

One of my ongoing frustrations with public engagement is the assumption in some corners that good public engagement means letting people recommend or promote any idea they want. Free from the bounds of real-world constraints, we let them spin their wildest ideas....and then, when they find out that we didn't recommend their ideas, they accuse us of "not listening."

Meanwhile, we roll our eyes and mutter about how "unrealistic" the public is.

I often refer to this as the Santa Claus approach to public engagement. I've been a good girl this year. I want a pony....and a rocket launcher... and a Ferrari...

Like most things that don't work as we intended, the root of the problem is in how we structured the engagement, because that's what set the stage for what we did. Teachers and business coaches know that generating effective creative ideas requires working within a structure. People need a realistic context, real-world sides on the box, if they are going to create something that is both new and useful.

If you don't believe me, try this exercise at your next staff meeting or coffee klatch:

Step #1: Ask people to list a number of ways in which they can use a brick. They can use it anywhere, anytime --there are no restrictions. Give them about a minute. Typical answers will involve using it as a paperweight, a door stop, or a weapon.

Step #2: Identify a specific place or context (e.g., in the kitchen, in a park, your kid's room) and ask the same people to list all of the ways they could use a brick in that place. For example, if "a kitchen" is the context, people may find uses like heating it up to make paninis, flattening a lump of dough, or using it as a trivet.

Step #3: Ask the group which approach – #1 (unbounded) or #2 (connecting to something) – yielded more creative solutions.

As Stephen Shapiro, my source for this exercise wrote,

> Nearly 90% of audiences choose the second way. In fact, when we take the time to evaluate the uses, there is indeed much greater divergence when using the second method. The first approach tends to yield a lot of common solutions.[23]

So we generate more creative ideas, and more directly usable ideas, when we ask people to think about solutions within a realistic content than when we just throw the doors open for ideas.

That means that if we want to honor and respect the time that our residents and business operators and others are giving us when we ask them to participate, we need to stop putting them in situations where all they can come up with are Santa Claus lists. Instead, we need to give them realistic situations to address meaningful challenges to try to solve. The opportunity to do something that will actually matter.

We owe them, and ourselves, a better experience than useless wandering.

---

[23]Stephen Shapiro, "Freedom Can Limit Innovation"
http://www.innovationexcellence.com/blog/2011/10/14/freedom-can-limit-innovation/

What we need is more, and better, arguing

I don't like to argue. My husband, the high school debate kid, will argue for the sheer entertainment of it. Sometimes I think he sparks political debates just for the entertainment of it. After 20 plus years, he does that less anymore, at least with me. When it comes to verbal debate, I'm not much of a match.

Clay Shirkey, a writer on journalism and new media issues, begins his TED talk[24] by demonstrating that throughout history, the development of new types of mass communication and the invention of new communication technologies have led people to believe that they were on the verge of new enlightenment. But every time, they got something other than the world peace that many hoped would result.

Instead, Shirkey explains, what we have gotten from every historic expansion of media has been...arguing. More arguing than existed before.

Shirkey particularly highlights the development of the scientific journal system. The Cliff Note version: as scientists began to print and disseminate their work in the 1700s, scientists also realized that they needed to create a system of review and vetting to maintain consistent quality and make sure that new science built on earlier discoveries. Printed books were helpful, but took too long to turn around; they needed something that would facilitate more timely review and quicker information-sharing. The result? The scientific journal,

---

[24] Clay Shirky: How the Internet will (one day) transform government [video]. Published September 25, 2012.
https://www.youtube.com/watch?v=CEN4XNth61o

with its regular publication, its relatively short articles and its emphasis on peer review.

As Shirkey points out, this communication innovation didn't lessen arguing – it facilitated more arguing over the validity of scientific studies that might have otherwise gone overlooked. What the scientific journal did create was *better* arguing.

Shirkey then shifts from the 18th century to the present – and to the present world of local government, one of the primary loci of arguing today. He points out that most current discussion of government "transparency" essentially proposes a one-way transaction. Transparency, through such efforts as open data initiatives, enables people to look into government's workings in a way that they have not previously, but that communication seldom goes both ways. As Shirkey puts it, "people with legislative power are not experimenting with participation." He likens public access to government data without two-way engagement to trying to drive a car that has a dashboard but no steering wheel.

The great need of the current era, Shirkey asserts, is for a new form of arguing – one that leverages the diffusing and connecting power of new communication technologies. And he suspects that we are only at the beginning of figuring out how our new tools will do that. But it's coming, he says, and we better figure it out.

——

So what will effective public engagement -- better, more meaningful, more constructive arguing – look like? And how will our new communication methods fit into it?

I don't have a magic answer (I'm kinda against those on principle...) but I think we are starting to figure out the basics. Here's what I think we need:

- We need a **structure** – a system for identifying the questions that we need to answer and solid methods for sorting through the options and identifying the best solutions. Our most popular current social media platforms can have a Wild West feeling to them, with only the barest of controls or ability to keep a conversation focused on an important outcome. If I want to maintain my social relationships, they work great – they're a valuable enhancement of the hang-over-the-fence-chat-with-your-neighbor. But hanging over the fence chatting is not how you would solve a problem in a conference room at work, and it's not how a teacher would make certain that you learned what you needed to learn. Rather than simply throwing conversations open, to let them wander where they will, we need tools that *design* and *channel* that experience, to get us to where we need to go.

- We have to have a **broad set of tools** and the **ability to pick the tool that will work best for each task**. Not everyone can express themselves in a written paragraph, or at a microphone. Not everyone wants to. Not every issue is explained best, understood best, worked on best, through words. We need to be able to grab and deploy the tool that works best for the specific challenge in front of us. Maybe that's a photograph. Maybe that's a user-created video. Maybe that's a map that anyone can put their mark on. Maybe that's something else. Instead of assuming that everything is solved through a written answer to the question or a multiple-choice survey, what other communication and collaboration methods can we put in their hands? In some ways, this is the great potential of online public engagement – if we can get past our assumption that everyone has a little Dostoyevsky trapped inside of them.

- Here is, perhaps, the biggest challenge: We have to have tools that create, that empower, the **two-way communication** that Shirkey was talking about. A survey is not enough. A comment page is not enough. Even "Idea Generation" - making big lists of bright or crazy solutions springing from the minds of our residents – isn't enough to create that two-way communication. It's still basically just information-gathering. It's nowhere near providing what we truly need. We need to be able to pull people into the process of evaluating the alternatives, playing a part in figuring out the solutions.

My deepest motivation for my interest in public engagement stems from this: in a complex, interdependent and unpredictable world, we need all the perspectives, all the experiences, all the brains we can get working on our community issues. If we are going to create wise economies, if we are going to endow our places with resilience and vibrancy for the long term, we need to crowdsource wisdom, not just bits of information.

We're starting to see the beginnings of a movement in this direction. But we have a long way to go before we get there.

I suspect Clay Shirkey ought to hang onto his notes from this talk for a while.

The Three D's of Terrible Public Engagement:

- **Descend on the community.** Come in as the expert outsider, believe that you know more than the people you are supposed to be engaging, tell them that until they believe it. Hint: you don't have to be a staffer of an international relief organization to Descend (and good relief organization staffers know how not to Descend). You just have to be enough wrapped up in some kind of inside ball – a pet urban design theory, your local zoning code, what happened in your town 30 years ago – to convince yourself that you know better on all points than anyone else who might be talking. Once you do that, you're Descending on the community – and the mistakes that might result from your blind spots are yours and yours alone.

- **Disconnect from the community.** Don't try to understand their context, or think about how successful engagement here will differ from what worked somewhere else. One size fits all is easiest, right? Until it blows up in your face. We can Disconnect just by unthinkingly sticking to a 19th-century approach despite our 21-st century residents.

- **Decide-Announce-Defend (or, be Dishonest).** The "public engagement" designed solely to check off the box on the regulation. The "Open House" with "feedback" for the project that is all but decided. No matter your country or your type of issues or type of community, we've all done this, been party to it, or been subjected to it. It's Defensive, and it's Dishonest. There's no way around that.

But perhaps more urgently, in a world where people have more and more access to information about our community and its issues, and where it's easier and easier for them to organize themselves to fight a proposal where their involvement wasn't wanted, Decide-Announce-Defend grows more and more risky. You might get away with a few situations where no one is paying attention, but if you don't learn to bring people to the table at the beginning, help them to be part of the solution, the chances that they will passively accept your Descending will only grow more and more slim.

What's the matter with social media?

Nothing. I'm a diehard Twitter/Facebook/LinkedIn user. I know some people have ambivalent relationships with this stuff. Not me. A day without checking my Twitter feed anymore feels like a visit to the Dark Ages. Just like when I started using email years and years ago – I simply cannot imagine life without it anymore. But as local government and community types start using social media tools more and more, I think it's essential for us to look at these with a clear, un-awed eye... and realize that what we need to do our jobs well probably requires much more than a Facebook page.

Social media platforms are tools. They're good for many uses, but - just like you can't drive a nail very well with a tape measure - there are things that each platform, as great as they are, simply cannot do well.

One of the things that standard social media platforms do pretty poorly is facilitate broad and meaningful public engagement in complex, messy situations.

I've written before about how public meetings that consist of an audience and a stand mic are, by and large, completely ineffective for enabling constructive engagement. The open format of a social media platform is basically just a bigger microphone. And if the human tendency to either dominate the floor or hide in the corner often ruins our ability to get anything worthwhile out of a public meeting, how much benefit can we realistically expect from the wide-open platform of a Facebook page or a Twitter stream?

Let me give you two examples, one from the local government world and one from... somewhere more fun. Let's start with local government.

The former mayor of Cincinnati, like most mayors, maintained a Facebook page. He and his staff used it to post information, announcements, pictures of local events, etc. A few years ago, he posted a picture of a very significant groundbreaking – the start of a streetcar line in Downtown Cincinnati. A very big deal, and a huge accomplishment for his administration. But an accomplishment that (like many accomplishments) has vehement opponents.

So what happened when he posted this happy picture? A quick succession of bitter comments rehashing the opposition to the streetcar effort. Which of course then generated equally nasty comments from trolley supporters (who are also equally vehement).

For about six hours, the level of vitriol in the comments on that picture crept toward nuclear detonation. Then someone from the Mayor's office apparently noticed what was going on and pulled the plug, but not before a lot of people had jacked up their blood pressure by a few notches. And not before another small but sad chapter was added to Cincinnati's struggles to have a rational discussion about an important issue.

The second example: my favorite band did a livestream broadcast of a concert to launch a new album. People like me (marginally nuts, admittedly) from all over the world were jumping up and down in front of their computer waiting for it to start. The company sponsoring the livestream also had a Twitter stream scrolling across the bottom of the web page, and tweets from viewers gushed in from all over the world.

About three songs in, the internet feed cut out entirely. Apparently a bad storm was wreaking havoc on the transmission. The Twitter feed at the bottom, though, kept running.... and the comments about the sponsoring company were not exactly what anyone would want associated with their name. In the end, the transmission was restored, we got to see most of the concert, and all was mostly right with the world... but even now, if you go to Twitter and look up the hashtag associated with the broadcast...let's just say that there's a lot in that stream that ain't going to show up in anyone's marketing campaign anytime soon.

Both of these anecdotes illustrate a critical challenge: If you simply open the floodgates, and you don't have adequate controls or channeling mechanisms in places, at some point you will get hit with a deluge – and there will be lots of things in the stream that you didn't want to run into.

If what we want to foster is a constructive, collaborative conversation that moves our community forward in a meaningful way, we have to become much, much more sophisticated than simply throwing up a Twitter hashtag and a Facebook page.

Meaningful conversations require effort to make and keep them reasonable – and we know from our public meeting experience and from our own lives that we as humans don't always put in this effort. When we do public engagement, for whatever reason, we need to actively manage the process – we have to support the people who are sincerely trying to be part of the solution and channel away from those more simplistic or less sincere tendencies that often scuttle our best intentions. We can do this. But we have to make the conscious effort. We have to do much more than stick a mic in the middle of the room, even if that mic is called "social media."

It will take a while...so you might as well get started

In a true display of democracy, a town hall meeting held at the New Bedford High School auditorium Monday gave the crowd of approximately 550 residents the opportunity to publicly voice every last one of the inane thoughts and concerns they would normally only have the chance to utter to themselves.

Though the meeting was ostensibly held to discuss a proposed $21,000 project to replace the high school's grass football field with synthetic turf, City Councilman Thomas Reed inadvertently opened the floodgates to a deluge of ill-informed, off-topic diatribes on inconsequential bullshit when he allowed those in attendance to demonstrate their God-given gift of language.

--"Town Hall Meeting Gives Townspeople Chance To Say Stupid Things In Public." *The Onion*, Sep 8, 2007.

(Everyone knows that *The Onion* is a satire/fake news website, right?

Right??

Just checking.)

—

In 2013, my son started a new high school. After a lot of deliberation, my husband and I decided to acquiesce to the kid's wish to attend an academically rigorous high school.

318

The kid was accepted in January. By the time he starts school in August, he will have had one Saturday morning with the music program, a one on one with an assistant principal, two weeks of band camp and a two day freshman orientation.

He had the meeting with the assistant principal last Saturday. It was not what I expected. There's my 14 year old, sitting across a conference table from a massive, intimidating-looking man - 300 pounds of tie-you-in-a-pretzel-if-you-mess-up. Generally a good trait in an assistant principal, thinks the former substitute teacher turned mom.

The assistant principal places a binder full of information in front of the kid. Mr. Intimidating then starts asking James questions (note that he had already been accepted). The questions start off with unsurprising stuff...what's your favorite subject in school, what do you do outside of school...easy for the kid to answer. Then, the questions take a surprising turn: what kinds of situations stress you out? How do you deal with stress? What are you passionate about -what gets you out of bed in the morning? If I asked your best friend to describe you, what would he say?

Find yourself a 14 year old boy and try those questions on him. Or try them on yourself.

James stumbles through them, and Mr. Intimidating takes notes.

Then the assistant principal asks James to open the binder. Sitting to the side, I steel myself for a marginally painful review of rules and requirements and consequences. Instead, Mr. Intimidating spends the next

20 minutes conversing with James about the core principles of the school's educational philosophy.

Critical thinking. Self-awareness. Compassion towards others. Integrity.

Deep stuff. Foundational stuff. Not a single rule or regulation.

As I listened, it dawned on me that this wasn't a one-off thing. It was just more obvious because of the setting. When my son did the music department event a couple of weeks ago, the entire group of kids ended by singing the alma mater. The incoming freshmen put arms around each other's shoulders, exactly the way the upperclassmen do, while they tried to read the words off a piece of paper.

Find yourself a 14 year old boy and try to get them to put their arm around the shoulder of another boy. Good luck.

And yet I watched my kid do exactly that.

—

Think for a moment about how we complain about the public's involvement in our planning and economic development and local government--in person and online. I opened this piece with a purposely over-the-top piece of satire, but...come on. Hits a little close to home, don't it?

We gripe that they don't behave themselves, that they say nasty or off topic things, that they pound soapboxes...or worse yet, that they just don't show up.

No wonder our meetings are so miserable. It's all their fault.

Now think for a minute about how much effort we've put into establishing our community's culture of public engagement. What have we -- and our predecessors-- done to convey, to demonstrate, what effective public engagement looks like? What have we done to set the tone, to establish the environment we want?

Do we even know what the public engagement we want looks like? Or would we sound like a 14 year old trying to answer a question about how his best friend would describe him?

What public engagement culture do we have?

If all James' new high school did was a 20 minute discussion of principles, I would never expect it to take. A 14 year old would forget that stuff before he got out the door. But when every aspect of the culture reinforces those principles-- alma mater sung with arms around each other, freshmen applauded by upperclassmen when they enter the assembly on their first day of school.

They're building a culture.

———

Put aside all that idealistic stuff about public engagement for a minute. Transparency, democratic process, people have a right to know... yah, yah. Got it.

For a moment, be purely selfish.

The fact of the matter is that we screw ourselves over when we don't have those conversations, when we don't build meaningful collaboration right at the beginning. We make the whole process of doing our jobs 47 times harder on ourselves than it should be.

The simple fact of the matter is that you know there's stuff that your community needs to deal with, and not dealing with it is compacting your budgets and your staff and your time to the point where the most basic parts of the job get harder and harder. You need things to change - better tax base, more efficient land use, less money getting sucked up into roads and pipes and programs that aren't generating a decent return on investment. And you know this is the case all over, so job-hunting or moving to a different town doesn't get you out of the mess.

People who don't stand in your shoes are not going to see the emerging issues that are self-evident to you. They're not going to intuitively understand what you're seeing any better than you're going to be able to anticipate what 3-D printing will enable 10 years from now.

And it's a psychological fact: when people don't have good information to work from, they over-rely on their past experience. "It worked just fine 10 years ago, just do it some more?" That's not an age issue or a gender issue. It's a human condition issue. And the only way to counteract that bias, that the future should look like the present, is to give our rational minds the information they need to shift their gears. That's the way human creatures work.

So why do most communities fail to have intelligent conversations about their futures?

———

We have a tendency to assume that The Public won't listen to reason. We point to lots of situations where residents say stupid things or make assumptions that, given the more extensive level of information we have to work with, just don't make sense. Even though we "told" them what the facts were, they "chose" not to listen.

Good teachers know that just telling someone something verbally doesn't mean it will stick in their head. That's why teachers don't just tell you something once. You hear it in a lecture, you read it in the book, you do a project, you write a paper. People need to interact with new information on multiple levels, and do that over time. If you want someone to understand something, just telling them doesn't cut it.

And yet, in local government, most of the time that's all we do. No wonder they can't mentally shift away from the status quo. No wonder they don't see the threats and opportunities we know about.

A fundamental purpose of our approach has to change. We have to become managers and facilitators of community conversations, not just presentation-givers, open-house-when-the-plan-is-all-but-done-holders, grouse-helplessly-to-each-other-when-they-don't-get-it-ers.

We can't keep falling back on "it's complicated...you wouldn't understand...trust us." And then wonder why people don't see the need for change.

Edward Deming, the father of modern manufacturing, gets quoted in business schools every day:

Culture eats strategy for breakfast and process for lunch.

—

In 2011 I wrote a blow-by-blow account of how I managed a potentially contentious public meeting. By 2012, that post has now been read by 3,500 people. Obviously that essay addressed something that a lot of people needed or wanted.

But keeping a meeting from blowing up....that's simply classroom management. That's the very basics. It's not creating a constructive environment. it's not enabling a constructive culture. It's not in itself moving us forward at all.

We have to change the culture of community participation, and we have to do it top to bottom. Organizations that take on culture change know that they have to do it intentionally...they have to build it into every interaction, every communication. They need to consciously reinforce the principles of the culture they want--not just by saying what the principles are, but living them through every interaction.

What are your community's public interactions telling people about how you want to relate?

What does the room setup say?

The rules...or lack of rules?

The options and opportunities for involvement?

Is meaningful public engagement built into your processes, beginning to end? How do you involve people upstream-- in setting policy and deciding priorities? Do people have real opportunities to be part of the solution, or do you just invite them in when there is a *fait accompli* to argue against?

Do you give them the ability to do something other than say no, no, no? Do you channel them into being part of the solution?

If you don't, don't despair. Culture change is a long and difficult process. That's why my son's new school starts on this work long before they get their books, and why they build it all the way through the experience. The more I think about it, I suspect it's not luck....it's got to be intentional.

———

Like most analogies, this one breaks down. A 14 year old, to at least some extent, goes where you tell him to go and does what you tell him to do. Especially if you are a 300+ pound assistant principal. But your residents will participate only if they perceive that the value of doing so will exceed the cost of their time and energy. Which makes a culture of meaningful public engagement all the more important.

So you might as well get started. Ask yourself: what would meaningful public involvement look like here? What do we need to learn from our residents? What do we want our public meetings to look, to feel like? What character, what principles do we want? How can we build that into everything we do?

It won't happen overnight. But goofy 14 year old boys don't turn into men overnight, either. So go ahead and get started.

Secret Weapon 3: Be Brave

Evolution or Revolution?

In 2012, one of my clients found themselves on one of those standing-on-the-precipice moments: In this project, are we creating an evolution, or a revolution?

They're well into the process of making revisions to some basic systems for how it does business, and the staff realized that they stood at a fork in the road. On the one hand, they could focus on cleaning up and streamlining the existing structure: improve the processes, fix some nagging problems, put in some cool new tools, but leave the fundamental paradigm intact. Continue on more or less as they had done for nearly 10 years. Evolve.

On the other hand, they could take this moment in time to completely remake the process, to do something fundamentally different that held out the promise of curing some deeper ills that had always seemed to be out of reach within the existing structure. Strike out on something new, potentially huge and largely unknown. Revolution.

Despite my occasional rhetoric, I'm not generally a damn the torpedoes kind of person. In most situations I can usually find both pros and cons to the status quo. Stability, institutional memory, consistency, lack of learning curve... those things matter, deeply. Especially for overextended, good-intentioned organizations tasked with the most difficult issues around.

That was the crux of the argument in favor of the evolutionary approach. After all, this agency had done a pretty significant overhaul of the same system a few years ago, and the memory of turmoil, confusion, angry struggles and uneasy compromises still hung in the air for many of them. Two staffers described how the work to finish the new/old system had been completed by a small group in a closed room....whose door didn't completely screen the shouting and crying from the rest of the office. For weeks.

You have too little staff, huge demands, some recently-closed wounds. Why would you want to tear it all open again?

Here's what amazed me and the other consultants working on this project: across the spectrum of people to whom we said, "Evolution or Revolution?" only a couple voted for evolution. Across the board, even among the people we thought least likely to want to strap on the armor, the response was the same:

We want a system that works better. Not a little better; much better.

Our community desperately needs new solutions, and we won't be able to do that with just tweaks to what we have today.

It's our responsibility to do the best we possibly can for the long-term good of our community.... And that means that we need to take on the revolution.

Revolutions are scary. These guys know that. They have scars. And they made the sober choice to go into a bigger battle despite what they have seen before.

Deciding to start the revolution can't be just a response to boredom or a cool idea in a magazine. A revolution takes bravery. And that bravery had to come from somewhere deep:

Deep knowledge of the place and its people.

Deep understanding that the existing structure, at its core, isn't doing what this place and its people deeply need.

Deep personal and professional integrity to admit that these are the facts of the matter.

Deep personal and professional bravery – the will to power to assert that this is the time and we are the people who have the opportunity to make it happen.

Making the choice for revolution is only a first step toward actually making meaningful change. They and we know that this could all fade in the face of opposition, leadership indifference, carelessness or fear. And I think everyone realizes that it probably won't come out in the end the way we might think it will, from where we stand today. But that choice – evolution or revolution – must be made if anything is going to get better.

I'm proud of these guys. Viva la revolution.

The first steps toward the marathon

It's a tough challenge that I keep pushing on you here. If you think that the realities of the world and communities around us require us to rethink, reboot and re-engage in the work of building great communities, it's easy to find yourself in the blind alley where those good intentions thump into a brick wall.

I started running last year after a lifetime of complete visceral aversion to anything having to do with fitness. As I was putting on my new shoes, my son asked me when the last time I had "run" anywhere was. He'd certainly never seen it. I racked my head, and the only thing I could come up with was elementary school gym glass, where Mr. Ridgeway, who must have weighed 300 pounds, would chase me while the class was running laps because I was far and away the slowest kid out there. I've always said that I only run when chased by something– that must be where I got it. Believe me, the picture in my head probably looks scarier than whatever you're imagining.

As a result of my complete lack of any sort of conditioning, calling what I do a "run" is like calling a kid on a tricycle Lance Armstrong. I still can't run a full 5k without stopping to catch my breath a couple of times. But I can run a mile without pause, and that's about 19/20th of a mile more than I could this time last year.

I keep saying that there are no magic bullets, and that we need to commit to the long, hard haul of incremental, deep-rooted, meaningful change. I can't take a pill to become a marathoner – I have to keep plugging at it, every day, bit by bit. And I have to start with the uncomfortable step of looking like a fat blob ker-plumping my way through the neighborhood, because without that start, I won't get anywhere at all.

Turning Pro

This passage is from Todd Henry's <u>The Accidental Creative</u>, an excellent read and podcast listen:

I spent much of my life as a paid amateur. I was doing what I needed to do to get the work done, but I was secretly waiting for someone to come along and "pick" me. I was saving myself for a marriage that would never arrive, while unwittingly giving myself over to anyone who came along. I worked hard, but I wasn't a pro. I was auditing my own life. I was a ghost.

In short, I lacked grit. I hadn't yet developed the "you will have to pry this work from my cold, dead hands" mindset to which I now aspire every day. My resolve wasn't yet steeled.

I remember the day it flipped. I went pro. I decided that I was going to do whatever it took to get my work out each day, and to develop my mind for wherever life led. The change was subtle, but it was marked by three little words that I swear are inscribed somewhere on the inside of my cerebral cortex: "Here I Stand."

Against the turmoil, *here I stand.*

Against the critics, *here I stand.*

Against the scoffers and cynics, *here I stand.*

Against my own fear, *here I stand.*

Against exhaustion, pettiness, and excuses, *here I stand.*

Against compromise and short-cuts, *here I stand.*

Against the seductive love of comfort, *here I stand.*

Here I stand, and neither your words, nor your threats will move me. I am a pro, and while I may not always produce great work, I produce, so deal with it.[25]

————

All of us who try to make communities better *are* creative professionals, in the purest sense of the word. Our mission is one of the most fundamental and noble: to make human communities better. We get mired in the details of meetings and projects and personality conflicts and politics, but you know what? So do people who do more conventionally "creative" work, like artists and writers. Creating is tough, whether it's a new painting, a new song or a new way of making local economies work.

Fear? Insecurity? Rejection? What else is new?

We need creativity in local governments, organizations, agencies. We need it more than ever. We need to embrace our own creativity, and that of our communities, if we are going to find solutions to those very tough questions, and more and more urgent. We need to claim our own commitment to working toward those answers within the messy world of everyday distractions and limitations if we're going to in any way be true to the good intentions of our choice to do this work.

We are conditioned to be part of a team, to stick with the instructions handed down by Them, to avoid rocking the boat if we can help it. If you work with local governments, elected officials, nonprofit boards of directors, etc., you've gotten that message over the years in no uncertain terms. It's no wonder so many of us give

———————————————

[25]Todd Henry, "On Turning Pro."
http://www.accidentalcreative.com/mindset/on-turning-pro/

up on that first impulse we had, to go into this work because it seemed like doing something that matters. After a few years of perpetuating a status quo that you know is limping, it's no wonder so many start counting the days to retirement.

A pro taps his or her own energy and commitment for the good of something bigger. You can't get bigger than what we deal with. We can't afford to be paid amateurs anymore.

The Divergent Creative and the Kid Who Won Everything Else

We need to be brave and creative and determined and all that. But you also know the other side: Sometimes your creativity only gets you cut.

I have two kids, who I've generally stereotyped as the Good Kid and the Mad Scientist. The older one has lots of great qualities -- good grades, well behaved, respectful, etc. Classic firstborn. Good Kid.

The second is... well, he's...yeah.

He's the one that leaves a trail of chaos in his wake. Remnants of projects and drawings and creations litter half the house. Fifty percent of all the food storage containers and reusable water bottles that cross our property line end up as bug habitats. Pretty much anything... scrap wood, tinfoil, sticks, silverware, you name it... gets conscripted into his projects. When he's working on something, he goes at it with a single minded devotion that verges on obsessive. Fat chance getting that dishwasher unloaded.

Granted, they're amazing projects. Yes, Mom is supposed to say that, but even given my bias...

The kid makes clay fish the size of your fingernail so detailed that you can identify the species. He makes reefs with dozens of types of corals that fit in your palm. He draws birds with all their plumage.

The kid has sold his work at art shows, exhibiting next to adults. He's been the youngest exhibitor every time. He's 11.

Today was Awards Day, the culmination of his years in elementary school. He won...nothing. The award for achievement in art went to the Kid Who Won Everything Else.

Jon knows how the quality of his work compares to his age peers. You can't help but notice at the school art shows. But he doesn't always do the art class project exactly the way he was told. Sometimes he figures he knows a better way. I don't know if he actually does know a better way or not. But he's usually quite sure of his vision.

—

I watched from the other side of the room as the teachers progressed through the awards. Jon congratulated his classmates...generous kid, sweet disposition. I watched him jump forward, then sit back down as a kid with the same first name as him was called to receive the science award (Jon's also a biology wizard, which explains the fish and the bugs and the birds).

But after the art teacher gave her award, Jon sank into himself as though someone had let the air out of his body. Across the gym, I tried to catch his eye, give a thin smile of encouragement, but he looked at no one.

After school, in the car alone, tears, dashed expectations, I try and try but I'm never good enough. Why don't they understand me? What's wrong with me?

Moms experience heart breaks that feel like nothing else in human experience.

———

I have an undergrad degree in education. About a year ago, bewildered about how to deal with this kid, I pulled out one of my old textbooks and reviewed the one chapter I could find on gifted education. The book listed six types of gifted kids. First up: standard good student. Check.

Second: Divergent Creative. Characteristics: independent thinker, resist playing by the rules, challenge authority, driven by deep need to create.

Student is at significant risk of tuning out of the education process.

Looky what I got.

———

The ironic thing here is that I started out as the Good Kid, but I think I turned into the divergent. I was the Kid Who Wins Everything when I was a kid. Now I'm the one who challenges authority, who ignores people at the community pool when I'm writing. Who says stuff that isn't popular with my peers. At least some of the time.

As much as the hyper-competitive in me wants him to Win Everything, I can't in clear conscience tell Jon to conform, do everything you're told, play the game without question. That's not true to me, and it's not true to him. And he knows that.

Kid is also pretty good at reading human behavior, including his own.

—

Why do we crave reinforcement? What makes us so desperate for praise, for approval, to hear that "good job?"

I don't know. But we have to make a choice sometimes: try to fit the system in the hopes of winning the award, or obey what we know, what we see, do what it seems like is our role in the world to do.

I think I have been evolving from Good Kid to Divergent because, fundamentally, I realized that I had nothing to lose. Job security is a myth, the ability to plan out a career like a stepping stone path continues to evaporate, hitching ourselves to dying stars seems like a poor exchange for good behavior and silence

Sometimes, though, that's a lonely and misunderstood path. Sometimes it simply feels like shit.

But it doesn't change who we are. Or what we have to do.

—

Ironically, I stumbled across a music video yesterday that I hadn't seen in years. It came out in 1993, by a band called Blind Melon, called "No Rain." It's the one with the little tap-dancing girl in the bumblebee costume who wanders around looking for her people and eventually finds a bunch of dancers in bumblebee costumes in a field.

Depending on your age, you either knew immediately what I was talking about or you have no idea. If you have no idea, just go with me for a moment. Or look it up on YouTube.

This one goes out to all you change agents, community leaders, Mad Scientists and tap dancing bumblebee people. Hang in there, guys

And as Jon told me after he got the tears out of his system, none of today's crap will matter a week from now. He'll try to play by the rules better, but he's not giving up what matters to him.

Wise kid, that Mad Scientist.

Boots and Saddles

My friends know that, if I come up with a quote that I didn't dredge out of my Twitter stream, it's most likely to come from one of two sources:

- Shakespeare (common ailment of English majors) or

- The Killers (rock band not particularly popular with English majors)

I have admitted publicly that I'm an embarrassingly big fan of that band, and I realize that blows my intellectual cred in some waters. But I find that they capture this combination of head, heart, spirit and determination that's been running through my work in the last few years, and they resonate deeply with me, more so than I ever thought a three-minute rock song could. They're probably the soundtrack of this book, and here's why.

Several years ago, the Killers had a big hit with a song that some people thought was maybe a little goofy. It has these lines in it:

> Are we human, or are we dancer?
> My sign is vital, my hands are cold.
> And I'm on my knees looking for the answer.
> Are we human, or are we dancer?[26]

People fussed a lot over the grammar of that first line, and in the process they seemed to miss the point. According to interviews, the human/dancer comparison derived from a quote from the author Hunter S. Thompson, in which he asserted that Americans were

---

[26] The Killers, "Human." © The Island Def Jam Music Group, 2008.

raising a generation of people who did what they were told without thinking about it (the "dancers," in Thompson's context).

What I love about the rest of the stanza and the song is the echoing of the question, the awareness of its implications, and the lack of a simplistic answer: the honesty and seriousness of the "I don't know."

I think that's the only legitimate response. Our recent history, and especially in how we have dealt with our communities, demonstrates that we have definitely been dancers. Are we making those mistakes again now? We have to keep asking that, but we also know that we can never be sure. We can only keep vigilance and live with that uncertainty, that ambivalence.

Sobering, kind of fatalistic stuff. If we can't know, why try?

The lead singer of the band wrote those words, and he was a 20-something kid at the time. In 2012, they came out with another album that in some respects seems to be a mature answer to that question - and the only honest answer I can come up with, either. One of the songs contains these words:

> What are we made of?
> Flesh and Bone.
> Am I running out of time?[27]

---

[27] "Flesh and Bone." The Killers/ B. Flowers, lyrics. © Universal-PolyGram Int. Publishing, Inc. (ASCAP), 2012

Not made of something powerful. Not made of something infallible. Flesh and Bone. The breakable, time-limited stuff. Uncertainty. Limited-ness. Weakness.

The song continues with this bridge section, in which the imagery shifts to the fear of a boxer in the ring making his debut (and then metaphorically trekking through the desert):

> This could decay, like the valley below.
> Defenses are down, stakes are high
> You scour the crowd for a face of compassion
> The grace of the journeyman fought is no more.
> The moment of truth and the roots of desire, [28]
> No neutral corners, just a compass and the sun.

After that moment, the music comes back in with furious guitars and drums - bambambambambam, and after another chorus, the song ends with a call to arms:

> Faces forward, and trade in
> This blindness for the glow of love.
> The time is raging, may it rage in vain,
> And you always had it, but you never knew
>
> So boots and saddles, get on your feet.
> There's no surrender, cause there's no retreat.
> The bells are sobbing in this monster land, [29]
> We're the descendants of giant men.

Here is what I love and have so deeply appreciated about this song during the time that I have been writing this book:

---

[28] *Ibid.*

[29] *Ibid.*

What should we do? What can we do? We don't completely know. We're often not going to know. We are dealing with messy, complicated stuff. We will not find easy answers.

If we're determined to make communities better in this era, we're going to have to flail about. We're going to have to take risks, we're going to have to put ourselves at risk of failure.

And we **are** going to fail (spoiler alert: the boxer in the song gets flattened).

What do we do, then, when we fail?

We get back up. We stay the course. We face forward, resolutely.

We remember why it matters.

Boots and saddles.

At the end of the day, I'm still optimistic. We are finding our way. All the trends I've talked about in this book are happening... often under the radar, often out of sight of the mainstream talking heads. But this hasn't been about creating a brand new movement or taking on challenges that no one has noticed yet. Your compatriots are out there, even if you don't know them yet. You will.

The real question is whether we ourselves become advance guards in the movement toward that future, or we flounder in fear and helplessness and resistance to the sea changes, and create an unnecessary dead weight on the future of our communities.

So boots and saddles, folks.

Boots and saddles.

Postlude:

The Bird Flip to Dying

Sometimes you have to force yourself to walk with your ghosts so that you know who they are. And who you are, too.

I always say that I am from Bedford, a small town outside Cleveland. But "from" might be the most telling word. After growing up deeply embedded in the community through my father and my grandfather and my own activities, I left that piece of the Rust Belt to go to college in Chicago. I came back for three summers, and then...

I left.

When my parents were alive, I would visit every so often. But not that often.

They died years ago. The last time I was in the house I grew up in, my brothers and I went through all of the furniture and dishes and tools and all of that detritus of a life, and divided it up. I continued to co-own that house with them for years, and my one brother still lives there.

I have never gone back inside.

—

I don't want to go back to my hometown anymore. I don't want to go back to the place that formed me, that played such an integral part in making me who I am that I put a picture of 1970s Cleveland on the introductory slide of every presentation I do.

It's one thing to talk about it. It's another thing to go there.

Don't get me wrong. It's a charming little Western Reserve Yankee kind of town. Lovely square with gravel paths and dignified war memorials, grand Victorian buildings around it. Gazebo that supposedly has a brick with my name on it somewhere (I've never found it... who knows if Granddad told the truth...he didn't always do that). Solid buildings lining Broadway. Stately houses on streets with real sidewalks. The Old Urbanism, Exhibit A.

But...

Drive around after a few years' absence, and you notice the potholes. You see the vacant lot where something's gone... what? I don't remember.

The post office on the site of the old Marble Chair factory – the one that shut down in the late 70s so abruptly that workers left their lunches on the tables. On that site, the post office looks too small.

Then drive through downtown and out into the non-quaint neighborhoods. Vacant storefronts. Empty buildings. Dried weeds in lots. Houses that might – or might not – have people living in them. Who might or might not be able to leave the house under their own power. You can't quite tell by looking.

There's a lot of that.

———

I went to Bedford, not wanting to visit my own ghosts, but to see a friend who has been visiting hers. One of my childhood buddies lost her mom a couple months ago. I had to skip the funeral, in the funeral home on the corner of the cemetery where my own parents are buried, because I had a cold/flu kind of thing. I wasn't all that sick, but I didn't want to risk infecting a room full of old people. You think about that in this context.

I felt guilty about not supporting my friend. And I did seem to have something. But I was kind of glad not to have to go.

I didn't want to go. I really didn't want to go.

My friend lives in Alaska. Seldom gets to Ohio. It's expensive. She came back for two weeks to help her Dad move and help clean out the house she grew up in. I promised I would come and see her. I figured a friendly face might do some good.

I stood in the front room of the tiny Cape Cod, the one that I could almost find without the address, although I hadn't been there in 25 years. The trees in the front had gotten bigger, which made the house look smaller than I remembered, and that threw me a little. But that wasn't as confusing at the thing that looked like a brick bunker at the end of the street -- that made me think I had taken a wrong turn.

Renee told me that the city had built that years ago to block off an alley – to keep drug dealers from the next town over from running their supplies down this little street.

The front room felt smaller, too, because of the boxes and bins and piles of papers and photos and phonograph records and who knows what else. I'd stood in rooms like this before, so I brushed off my friend's apologies. I've been there, don't worry about it, this doesn't look too bad, you've made a lot of progress. I know. It'll be OK.

When you sit there in the middle of all of that, with the ghosts of your own long-ago life racing around you disjointedly, you don't know if you will ever get done. Or if it will ever be ok.

———

Later that day, I made the call that I didn't want to make. I called my brother, the one that still lives in the house where we grew up, who lives there alone and survived a long period of unemployment by selling off almost everything that my other brother and I didn't claim. Knowing how little he had, we didn't claim much.

The one who never visits, never talks, with whom a 15 minute phone conversation feels like a mental battle to say something not stupid.

I apologized for the short notice, said I hadn't known sure that I was coming until earlier that day (that was true – my friend had been sick), and asked if he had time to go grab dinner. He said yes. I hadn't talked to him for over 8 months.

I proposed to meet at a little pizza shop that I had noticed on the way through town – in the storefront that used to hold the magazine shop at the foot of our street. Two doors down from the newspaper where I had my first job, across the street from the shop where I got my first haircut.

The ghosts swirled. I couldn't get any closer to the house.

Brian walked down the street, met me on the corner, hug. It's 8:30, pizza shop looks like it's closing, everything else around is dark except for a bar (he doesn't drink). We get in my car and go to Applebee's out past the high school, just this side of the shopping mall where I bought my first record, where I wrote a big feature spread for the paper when the mall turned 30 or 40 or something. The place that I was warned after college not to go near, because I was sure to get mugged. I forget who told me that.

I mostly remember how to get there, but have to double-check myself with him a little. He has lived in Bedford for most of his 41 years, never lived farther than an hour from here. He doesn't have that problem.

Under the pendant lamp at the Applebee's booth, Brian looks a little less thin than he used to be. I am probably thinner than the last time I saw him – I was supposed to run my first 5K tomorrow, but cancelled that to come here. We have the same face, primarily our dad's face. Same hair, same shape, same wrinkles, even the same cleft lip scar, except that his is the mirror image of mine.

Same eyes.

Brian talks some about his job, asks politely about my kids, but talks for a long time about the church we grew up in. They're losing population fast, can hardly afford to pay a pastor. When we were kids they had two pastors, and two parsonages. They sold the one next door back when our dad was the church council president. Now they are looking at a merger with three or four other churches, most of which are even smaller. There's no one left except old folks. Brian says he's the only one in his generation who shows up on Sunday. And in a brief flash of something interior, he says: "This is the church I grew up in. I don't want to see it die."

There's a sadness in his eyes all the time. He hasn't had it easy. That sadness intensifies in that second.

I drive him to the house I grew up in, note in the dark that it's still standing, nothing obviously wrong, landscaping is overgrown. Hug, goodnight, let's do a better job of staying in touch. A string of apologies from me. He doesn't invite me inside. I head for a hotel downtown – I've scheduled a meeting with a colleague in the morning.

At the hotel, I look in the mirror. And notice, not for the first time, the way my eyes look vaguely sad when I am not talking to someone.

—

"What kind of culture lets this happen to its cities? How are people okay with the post-apocalyptic Mad Max hellscape that is Detroit?"

One of my Twitter correspondents runs a regional planning agency in Akron. He has been reading *Detroit: An American Autopsy* by Charlie LeDuff. Jason lives the Rust Belt experience every day, and he thinks deeply.

I checked my Twitter over breakfast before leaving for Bedford. This book is clearly working him over. I read the review he tweets.

Cringe.

I don't add the book to my reading list.

—

Driving out of downtown Cleveland heading home after my last meeting, I glance sideways from I-90 to glimpse the Detroit-Superior Bridge over the Cuyahoga Valley. That's the two-decker one – the one that 70 years ago carried streetcars on its lower level. That level hasn't been used for decades.

My father, the self-taught paint chemist who always had bigger dreams that never happened, used to talk to me about his vision for a tourist experience in that lower level – a little fragment of streetcar track and a car to take people out over the river valley to take in the view and get a snack in the old canteen at the stop down there. He even took me at some point when someone did a tour of that lower level – I forget whether I was in college or if that was after I got married. I didn't realize then that his love of places like that – and his inclination to proclaim "I see usability" - would have a profound impact on my career.

The space was dark, full of debris, lit by only sunlight. But it was a hell of a view.

It's still not used, except for once in a while when someone holds an art fair or something like that on the old streetcar level. I haven't been, but my other brother, an illustrator, exhibited there once. He says it was fun – all sorts of dance and performance art under temporary lights run off generators and extension cords.

I just bought one of his local prints from a proud-of-everything-Cleveland shop downtown. It's the names of the city neighborhoods arranged in the shape of the city. I told myself that I bought it so that I could keep track of where the neighborhoods are if I end up with a consulting gig in Cleveland. But I don't really know why I bought it, other than I like his work and I want to support my niece and nephew…and this little store.

Random quote in my head: A violin in the void. Vladimir Nabokov, describing his stories about dislocated Russian exiles before and after World War II.

I tell myself that's the wrong quote for Cleveland, the Comeback City.

———

Past the bridge, it's a minute or two until I pass the remaining steel mills – I catch the old familiar scent, but it's not the overwhelming miles-away smell I remember. Then into a grey landscape of highway, warehouses, suburbanish buildings, more spread apart buildings. A landscape eventually dominated by the dark grey trees and brown grass of late Ohio winter. I debate turning on the radio, but end up talking to myself instead.

Why does this place feel like the Valley of the Shadow of Death? Am I just doing some kind of long-suppressed grieving – for parents who died too early, for tenuous family ties, for roots that have mostly shriveled, for my own realization that my time slides away?

Is it Renee in her family detritus?

Is it Brian struggling to hold together the family that I have never been for him, in the face of a community where old people die or move away, and new people never come?

Is it potholes, vacant stores, vacant lots – the physical in-my-face manifestations of all of the grim statistics and trends that I have read so long, that I know so well? I follow news from Cleveland, from Detroit, from Buffalo, and so on, pretty closely – I am From Here, after all.

Is it Jason's anguish for Detroit, for its sister communities that he works so hard for, seeing in the brutal struggles of Detroit a mirror or a prophecy for the places he cares about?

That I still care about?

—

What audacity animates the people who are trying to build something in places that struggle – the hundreds of people that I know, or that I know of, who are working in some way to turn hard-time communities around? The people who fly in the face of Where the Market Looks Good to open a shop in a struggling neighborhood, or run a downtown revitalization program, or crowdfund a container park, or make pictures that show happy local landmarks? The people who do the art thing under the bridge?

People like Tony, Kristen, Taylor, Chris, Mark, Jennifer?

People like Jason?

I used to do that – I helped start a downtown revitalization program for a downtrodden neighborhood in Wisconsin, when I lived there in my 20s. I still talk to and advise and support and encourage people all over the country who are trying to make their places better.

But I don't do it myself anymore. Where I live now, no one needs me for that. And I confess that I don't seek it out. I know how exhausting it is. I touch it enough every day to make that hard to forget.

In some ways, it's very easy for me to encourage people to be brave. If it were easy, you'd have already done it, I tell them. Go get 'em – go make it happen.

How do you maintain that bravery in the face of decline – decline that is everywhere you look, decline that runs through all community systems? Decline that goes back decades, decline all around? How do you maintain it for the months and years and decades where you take a step forward and then (if you're lucky, only) a half-step back?

———

The morning after my visits with Renee and Brian, while I was still standing in a hotel room that had been created from an old bank building on Euclid Avenue, Jason tweeted this passage from the same book. When a quote matters so much to someone that they send it despite having to divide it into five tweets, you know that they think it matters:

#1 "The small, white 'art community' in Detroit complained that I was focusing on the negative in a city with so much good. What about (ctd)

#2 "all the galleries and museums and music? they complained in a flurry of emails and blogs. What about the good things? (ctd)

#3 "But these things are not supposed to be news. These things are supposed to be normal. And when normal things become the news, the (ctd)

#4 "abnormal becomes the norm. Writing about shit like that [galleries and museums] in the city we were living in seemed equal to (ctd)

#5 "writing about the surf conditions while reporting in the Gaza Strip." -Charlie LeDuff "Detroit: An American Autopsy"

I felt like I should respond. But I had no idea what to say.

———

When we love a person – a parent, a spouse, a friend, a sibling – we know that we love something that is imperfect. We know where the bad stuff is, where the baggage lies. We have a clue where the dark places sit and at least a little bit of an inkling of what might be in there.

We choose to love despite knowing that.

Sometimes the bad stuff is too much and we walk away. But when we do choose to love someone, we know that that's going to be there. And we're going to just have to live with it.

But why do we ever make the choice to live with it?

I'm no psychologist, or pastor, or much of an expert on anything along these lines. I often wonder how my husband and I managed to marry at such a young age and not completely botch it up. And I'm not sure how much credit I get for the fact that somehow we haven't.

But rolling across the grey highway among the grey trees, asking my urgent question out loud in the empty car – "why should anyone keep trying to make a place better, when the whole system seems to be falling apart?" something managed to dawn on me:

When we love someone, we focus on what's good about them. We know the bad stuff is there, and we try to help them with it, but that's not what we choose to see first.

If you ask me about my husband, I will tell you about his kindness, his maturity, his self-assurance, his wisdom. I'll withhold the arrogance and the impatience, or make a joke out of them. Hopefully he does that for me.

———

The work of setting up art shows, or fighting for better transportation systems, or cleaning up neighborhoods, or opening businesses, matters. It matters furiously. It matters a hell of a lot.

It matters because it shows us why these places are loved. And it shows us that somebody loves them, deeply loves them. Which means that it's OK for us to love them. Despite everything.

It says: there is something, something profound, something deep here that Matters. The ugly, the despairing, the potholed... loving a place doesn't negate those facts, or negate the need to fix them.

But our efforts at revitalization, however short of the Everything This Place Needs, allows us to see what's good about it, what there is here that can engender that love. And it allows others to see that. And it allows us to connect to the place down in our hearts that wants to love our places ourselves.

I finished this book in northern Wisconsin, my other old stomping grounds. On the way here, I drove through a tiny town, not even a town, not much more than a crossroads with five or six buildings. No local government any closer than the county seat.

I saw a 30-foot sign on a slight hillside, thousands of colored stones, neatly arranged: "ALASKA, WI."

First thought: someone gives a damn about this place.

—

Richard Rodriguez, probably my favorite author, wrote a stunning essay in a book titled *Brown: the Last Discovery of America*. You don't realize this until the end, but the essay is about the death of his friend, a difficult and drawn out death, from cancer. In one of those passages that you don't know what it's about until you've read the whole thing, he writes:

> Adam and Eve were driven by the Angel of the Fiery
> Sword to a land east of Eden, there to assume the
> burden of time, which is work and death. All
> photosynthetic beings on earth live in thrall to the
> movement of the sun, from east to west....We know our
> chariot sun is only one of many such hissing baubles
> juggled about, according to immutable laws.

> Fuck immutable laws. Fuck mutability, for that matter.
> I just had my face peeled. I go to the gym daily. I run.
> I swallow fistfuls of vitamins. I resort to scruffing
> lotions and toners. Anywhere else in the world I could

pass for what-would-you-say? In California I look fifty.

Of course he realizes the ultimate ineffectiveness of his face peels and toners. But he offers no apology for them.

And taking that stance in the face of knowing that mutability – flipping the bird to the universe - it does not stop death, but it asserts that Something Matters, despite it.

———

Communities are not people – they live longer than any one person, and in most places, they never truly go away. Cities in even struggling parts of Europe and Asia date back hundreds or thousands of years. So personifying a place – comparing it to a person you love or your own mortality– only works so far.

When you strive to make a community better, you are doing something that will have repercussions long past your own lifetime. No one who built the Detroit-Superior Bridge, or the Civil War memorial on the square in Bedford, or the house where I grew up, is still alive. But the impact that those places have continues past its first humans. Keeping those places working, maintaining and re-creating their relevance, empowering other people to take care of them and themselves, all of these things Matter. They matter a hell of a lot.

---

[30] Richard Rodriguez, *Brown: The Last Discovery of America.* Penguin Books, New York. Location 2407 (Chapter 8)

Maybe what you do to revitalize your place is a violin in a void. But maybe the violin in the void changes the void. Maybe it eventually fills the void, makes the void no longer empty. Maybe it enables the void to become something else. Or maybe all you're doing is flipping the bird to a world that says your place is dying.

And since places are not people, maybe you're making that happen.

Fuck Mutability.

To those of you who fight this good fight, go get 'em. And thank you.

About the Author

Della G. Rucker, AICP, CEcD

Della Rucker consults, speaks and trains on economic revitalization and public engagement for local governments and community organizations across the United States. She is one of a small number of private sector professionals to carry the industry-standard certifications in both planning and economic development.

Della is Principal of the Wise Economy Workshop, a consulting firm. She also writes for several professional publications and serves as Managing Editor of *EngagingCities,* an online magazine that focuses on the intersection of web technologies and public engagement. She produces podcasts and videocasts for the Wise Economy Workshop, *EngagingCities* and *PlannersWeb.*

A former English teacher and journalist, Della holds a bachelor's degree from Northwestern University in Chicago and a masters in community planning from the University of Cincinnati. She lives in Cincinnati, Ohio, with her husband and two sons.

You can follow Della on Twitter @dellarucker, find original writing at <u>wiseeconomy.com/blog</u> and listen to podcasts at <u>soundcloud.com/wiseeconomy</u>.

End Notes

www.ingramcontent.com/pod-product-compliance
Lightning Source LLC
Chambersburg PA
CBHW050643270326
41927CB00012B/2850